D1131012

HALLS OF HONOR

ROBERT F. PACE

HALLS OF HONOR

COLLEGE MEN IN THE OLD SOUTH

LOUISIANA STATE UNIVERSITY PRESS

BATON ROUGE

Copyright © 2004 by Louisiana State University Press
All rights reserved
Manufactured in the United States of America
FIRST PRINTING

DESIGNER: Andrew Shurtz
TYPEFACE: Adobe Caslon
TYPESETTER: Coghill Composition Co., Inc.
PRINTER AND BINDER: Thomson-Shore, Inc.

LIBRARY OF CONGRESS CATALOGING-IN-PUBLICATION DATA

Pace, Robert F.
Halls of honor : college men in the Old South / Robert F. Pace.
p. cm.
Includes bibliographical references and index.
ISBN 0-8071-2982-8 (hardcover : alk. paper)
1. Male college students—Southern States—History—19th century.
2. Education (Higher)—Southern States—History—19th century.   I. Title.
LA227.2.P33 2004
378.1′981′0975—dc22
2004011046

Honour and shame from no condition rise;
Act well your part, there all the honour lies.

—ALEXANDER POPE (1688–1744),
Essay on Man

Contents

Acknowledgments

It is a pleasure to acknowledge the many people who helped bring this project to completion. The bulk of my initial archival research occurred through the generosity of two consecutive Summer Research Grants from Longwood University, Virginia.

I want to express my appreciation to the wonderful professional staffs of the various archives and libraries I visited. I thank them for permission to quote from and reproduce materials from their collections. I am also indebted to Library Director Calvin Boyer and the interlibrary loan office at the Longwood University Library, and to the director of the Jay-Rollins Library at McMurry University, Joe Specht, and his interlibrary loan librarian, Terry Young.

I will be forever thankful to a wide variety of scholars and colleagues who have read and commented on various drafts of this book over the years. Throughout this project, I had tremendous encouragement and advice from my mentor and friend Grady McWhiney, whose example as a scholar and teacher I hope to someday emulate. At Longwood University, James R. Munson and L. Marshall Hall read several drafts and always gave sage advice about thesis and direction. Bill Harbour, James Crowl, Maurice Sneller, and Gilbert "Jack" Millar also encouraged my further study of concepts of honor with a wide variety of contextual readings. Christopher A. Bjornsen, a developmental psychologist, helped me explore the vast literature about adolescent development.

At McMurry University, I have had the great privilege of advice and friendship from some excellent colleagues. Robert Sledge and Robert Wettemann read the final manuscript and had several important suggestions. Gary Shanafelt, an expert on the Austro-Hungarian Empire, assured me that he could only provide copyediting suggestions because this book is so far away from his field. Fortunately for me, he proved himself wrong when he made some of the most important contributions to my conclusions. Donald S. Frazier, whom I met in graduate school fifteen years ago, has become like a brother to me. His advice, friendship, and example have made this a better book, and me a better scholar.

I would also like to acknowledge the assistance of the LSU Press in making this book. Sylvia Frank Rodrigue encouraged the project from the early stages through the finished product. I also want to thank the Press's anonymous outside reader, whose questions and suggestions helped me to refine and strengthen my arguments.

I owe a tremendous debt to my family. My parents, Rudy and Joyce, and my in-laws, George and Kaye, have always supported me in all that I do. My sister, Joy, and my brother, Dolph, have both inspired me with their energy and talents. I also want to thank my daughter, Catherine, who, at age eight, sat in my lap and typed at least two pages of this book so she could be a writer, too. She makes me proud every day. And finally, I want to thank my wife, Jill, whose intelligence, grace, and patience are matched only by her steadfast support through the years.

HALLS OF HONOR

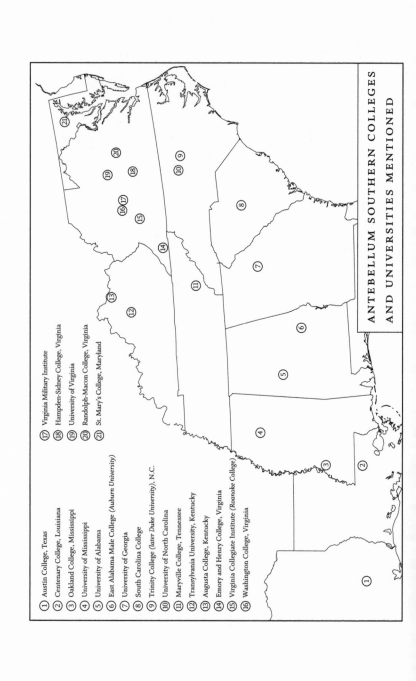

ANTEBELLUM SOUTHERN COLLEGES
AND UNIVERSITIES MENTIONED

1. Austin College, Texas
2. Centenary College, Louisiana
3. Oakland College, Mississippi
4. University of Mississippi
5. University of Alabama
6. East Alabama Male College (Auburn University)
7. University of Georgia
8. South Carolina College
9. Trinity College (later Duke University), N.C.
10. University of North Carolina
11. Maryville College, Tennessee
12. Transylvania University, Kentucky
13. Augusta College, Kentucky
14. Emory and Henry College, Virginia
15. Virginia Collegiate Institute (Roanoke College)
16. Washington College, Virginia
17. Virginia Military Institute
18. Hampden-Sidney College, Virginia
19. University of Virginia
20. Randolph-Macon College, Virginia
21. St. Mary's College, Maryland

Introduction

A FEW YEARS ago, as I sat in the reading room of the Southern Historical Collection at the University of North Carolina at Chapel Hill, I became hopelessly diverted from my original task by a fascinating collection of letters. What had caught my attention was a series of correspondence from the late antebellum period between Andrew McCollam Jr., a student at Centenary College in Louisiana, and his parents. I found myself caught up in McCollam's description of his life at college—his hopes and fears; his favorite academic subjects; his homesickness; his friends; and his struggles to establish himself as an adult. When he returned home a few years later, he was no longer a child, but a man of the world.[1]

What struck me about McCollam's letters from more than a century ago was that there was so much familiar about the struggles of adolescence in leaving home for the first time; but college in the Old South also represented something different from the familiar. Reserved almost exclusively for the sons (and some daughters) of the wealthiest planters, college life was not a representative existence for most southerners. I wanted to be able to understand what motivated these young men and women. What forces helped to determine their behavior, attitudes, and accomplishments? After all, these students would become the future economic and political leaders of the region. How, then, did their college experiences shape *them*, and how much did their society shape their college experiences?

In my search to answer these questions, I pursued two major lines of inquiry: 1) what have other scholars said about college life in the Old South? and 2) what can primary sources tell me? The answers to those questions have resulted in this book—a new look at the college student experience in the Old South.

First, let me discuss what others have said about college students in the antebellum South. In 1928 E. Merton Coulter published *College Life in the Old South,* which would shape an understanding of higher education's role in creating southern leadership for generations. Coulter focused his study on the University of Georgia, arguing that the southern college community conformed to definable "type," and that there "were no fundamental differences in what happened" at major southern universities. The typical college student that emerges from Coulter's pages is a member of the southern aristocracy, who "took the business of going to school seriously, although he worked just as hard in doing mischief called forth by an educational system which took its students young and which in dealing with them considered them still younger."[2] Although I agree that it was possible for southern college students to be similar across the region, using the experiences from one institution, the University of Georgia, to support this thesis always seemed less than satisfactory to me.

In more recent years numerous scholars have offered expanded views of southern college life. Most colleges and universities have an official history, and most of them provide small glimpses of college life in between long, dry accounts of the activities of presidents, trustees, and faculty. In 1987, however, Helen Lefkowitz Horowitz broke new ground in her sweeping treatment, *Campus Life: Undergraduate Cultures from the End of the Eighteenth Century to the Present.* This work attempts to describe how college students' lives have evolved in the United States since its founding. Horowitz has produced a very present-oriented work, beautifully crafting the story of how modern campus life came to be. Her main focus is that collegians have not been homogeneous; in fact, there has been a steady development of different groups on college campuses since the end of the eighteenth century. She asserts that, through her research, she has found "three distinct ways of being an undergraduate, with their male and female variants: college men and women, outsiders, and rebels." Of the three, she argues, college men and women and outsiders were prominent in the period before the Civil War.[3]

College men and women were the insiders, the creators of campus life. According to Horowitz, this campus life "was born in revolt." She asserts that at all colleges the wealthier students broke the rules and led revolts. In general, the nineteenth century brought the growth of a "genteel" temperament, which was the result of wealthier families creating individualized, self-indulgent children. Genteel sons were "pleasure-loving" and "extroverted." Colleges and universities, however, were led by presidents and faculty who were of an earlier era, with a different outlook on life. They were of the "evangelical temperament," and they expected the students to be submissive. The student revolts, therefore, resulted from a clash of values between the students and the faculty and were about power. In the violent and open revolts, the students often lost, but they then turned their resistance and protest into more subtle opposition through the creation of literary societies, social fraternities (primarily in the northern colleges), and other extracurricular activities. These endeavors, asserts Horowitz, created "college life" in the United States.[4]

Another student archetype, according to Horowitz, is the "outsider." These were the pious, studious students. They recognized the fun of college, but were more serious about the role that college played in their lives. They worried about the future and saw college as a preparation. They would become the ministers, the professors, or the college administrators in the future generations. These students, writes Horowitz, "lived in an oppositional culture, in the shadow of the dramatically visible fraternity and club structure. They learned a sharp lesson that served them well about the location of wealth and power. As they coped and struggled outside the prestigious world of the insiders, they found the kinds of rewards open to brains and to sustained effort. Good grades, which the college man scorned, emerged as a means to graduate fellowships and to professional training. It was not a glamorous life, but its hardness, cruelties, and achievements had a tangible quality that ultimately paid off."[5]

Horowitz's "ways of being an undergraduate" do seem to fit a general evolutionary pattern for the development of modern campus life, but student life in the Old South does not conform comfortably to her model. Student "insiders" and "outsiders" did exist, but, as she admits, the college student body of the Old South was more homogeneous.

Southern college students were, overwhelmingly, from the wealthier strata of society. The result was that social fraternities and similar organizations, which began in the North, did not develop as rapidly in the South. There was no need. All students were considered social peers, and this is where the generalization breaks down. Of course there were some students who valued learning more than others, but these students, as often as not, were also major players in creating "college life" in southern institutions. Southern students fall outside of the Horowitz model in other areas as well. For instance, she asserts that college men insisted that "scholastic rank carried no prestige" and that these students had no real interest in getting to know faculty, inside or outside of classes. A thorough review of student letters and diaries, however, refutes both of these claims for the antebellum South.[6]

Despite these differences, Horowitz still makes the important point that not all students were alike in their paths through college. Although the overwhelming majority of southern students were from the wealthiest families, not all of them were destined to become prominent slaveowners themselves. Students at many of the sectarian colleges in the South intended to enter the ministry or the professions. To a lesser extent, the same is true of those who entered state universities.

The point of this book is not to explore the reasons for entrance into college. Neither is it to study the evolution of curriculum, the changing nature of faculty and college administration, the role of the college and university in creating southern society, or the development of higher education in the nation. These are all interesting and well-documented topics; but for this book, they will only be discussed in relation to its major purpose—to understand the *culture* of being a college student in the Old South.

What becomes clear through my second line of inquiry—a search through thousands of primary sources—is that this student culture was created through a collision of two major forces: the southern code of honor and natural adolescent development. The concept of honor that governed Old South society was, at times, a difficult and confusing code. Southern honor consisted of a set of rules that advanced the *appearance* of duty, pride, power, and self-esteem; and conformity to these rules was required if an individual were to be considered an honorable member of society. Nor were these rules confined to a particular class or social group; honor was an intricate part of the entire southern society.[7]

The rules that governed southern honor, though complex, can be explained rather simply. Being a man of honor in the South meant that one exhibited a persona that conformed to the society's expectations. Appearance superceded content. In public, southern men had to exhibit behavior that held them to be dutiful to their responsibilities, respectful of their peers, and, most of all, honest in their public declarations. This ethic, however, did not say that one actually had to *be* dutiful, respectful, or honest; one simply had to *appear* to be a man of duty, respect, and honesty. Any public hint that a southern man was anything contrary to this definition had to be challenged rapidly and publicly in order to maintain the identity of a man of honor.

Southern honor stretched across all class boundaries. The southern gentry effected their practiced public images with style and grace. If any challenged this image, the result could be a defense of this persona on the dueling field, because a man of honor was expected to be willing to defend his public face with his life. The rules of honor, however, also permeated the lower classes of the region. Challenges may have resulted in knife fights or family feuds, but the causes and results were often the same.

Young men entering southern colleges in the antebellum era grew up immersed in the more genteel versions of this code. It influenced their development in ways that were qualitatively different from their other childhood experiences. Handed down by parents and other influential adults, the honor code was a set of rules and behaviors to be absorbed and used in a relatively mechanical fashion. Children are able to understand and apply concrete facts and rules of social convention. As they reach adolescence, however, their cognitive abilities change substantially and they are able to think in abstractions. With the average age for entering college in the antebellum South being fifteen, these young men were just beginning to be able to use the code of honor in more intentional and creative ways, while also constructing their own versions of the ethic, applicable within their peer group.[8]

For these young men, honor was the framework that gave shape to the more natural ambivalence of adolescence. Adolescence is not a sturdy, straight bridge between childhood and adulthood, but a transition fraught with conflicts and struggles. One of the major struggles was the drive to become an adult while retaining childhood desires and behaviors. Students enjoyed their newfound freedom away from home, but often expressed this independence through childish pranks and unfettered revelry. These behaviors vacillated frequently between immaturity and what the students perceived to be adult reactions. A second critical struggle for antebellum college men was the need to become a part of the culture of their authority figures, while also creating an "adult" culture of their own that focused on their peer group and involved a peer-designed code of honor.

It can be argued that class also played a significant role in shaping student behavior in the nineteenth century. In the South, it is certainly true that students came from the upper classes. Nevertheless, it was the code of honor, more than privilege, that guided the very existence of young students. Conflicts arose not through power struggles alone, but through perceived breaches of the code. Faculty and presidents in the South, many of whom were native northerners, did not always understand this code, and that is where the struggle ensued. L. Ray Drinkwater writes of these northern faculty members: "Among Puritanism's legacies was a code of human deportment that exalted reserve, not ostentatiousness; that saw material success as a manifestation of God's blessing, not as a means to obtain the admiration of men; that subordinated the need for public approval and respect to the inner satisfaction of knowing that one's actions were proper; and that revered self-control rather than self-assertion." According to Drinkwater, even southern-born faculty members tended to side with their northern colleagues on these issues.[9]

The relationship between students and faculty becomes more clear, however, through the words of student letters, papers, diaries, and speeches. Although it is true that many students taunted faculty, there was also a general sense of respect for the professors as learned men. There were, of course, many cases of a "we versus they" syndrome between students and faculty, but it was a normal function of adolescence in asserting a push toward independence. Therefore, when this antagonism moved from the realm of covert defiance to outright rebellion, as it certainly did throughout the period, it was not because the students necessarily believed themselves to be socially superior to the faculty. The resistance, in almost every case, stemmed from students perceiving that their honor—the code that maintained their very existence in the southern society—had been breached.

This argument is not to say that northern students were without honor; they simply were not held to the society-wide ethic under which all southern students dwelled. Students of means in the North believed that their class status demanded a level of respect and dignity, but there was a wider variety of social classes in northern colleges and universities. This class disparity helped lead the wealthier students to both make demands of the faculty, locking them into the power struggles described by Horowitz, and to separate themselves from students of lower classes through exclusive social organizations. In his history of Harvard, Samuel Eliot Morison asserts that the typical Harvard men of the nineteenth century were "boys from New England families of middling fortune, and the swells were outnumbered by the horny-handed lads from the country districts, 'fitted for college' and provided with a scholarship through the efforts of the local minister."[10]

Differences between northern and southern students abounded. While few southern students had opportunities for scholarships, even the small handful who did not come from the wealthiest planters had to uphold their honor as peers in the college environment. Honor created a more conformist society in the South than in the North. According to Bertram Wyatt-Brown, "All traditional societies, the slaveholding South among them, provided little space for the individual, at least by present-day standards of privacy. Tradition has it that no man or woman ever was—or should—be an island. Instead, one's existence and even one's capacity or right to survive are determined in the public forum— the *deme* or larger 'family' of peers and superiors called community. Deviance from accepted norms can only be tolerated if the offender somehow conveys a sense of powerlessness. Otherwise the nonconformist, whose misdeeds may be real or socially conjured up, faces ostracism or worse."[11] This conformity, or breaches of it, therefore, were the catalysts of student rebelliousness in the South. Of course revolts in the South, as in the North, were about power, but not *just* about power. The genesis of these revolts lay in the southern student adherence to a code of honor—their public face. They could not allow anyone, whether professor or classmate, to impugn their honor, no matter how incidentally.

Honor in the South, according to Peter Bardaglio, was "that constellation of ideas and values in which one's sense of self-worth rested on the degree of respect commanded from others in the community."[12] Challenging students' honor was tantamount to challenging their self-concept, and that challenge need not be serious for it to be taken seriously. "All insults were equal in the sense that they implied that [one] had been reduced to a slavish condition," writes Kenneth Greenberg. "Honor and dishonor, like mastery and slavery, were total conditions." Understanding these conditions was part of life in the South, and remnants of this collective knowledge have remained as a difference between North and South well into the modern era.[13]

Of course, rebelliousness among college students in the nineteenth century was not restricted to American universities; indeed, student unrest and rebellion helped to transform the face of European history. Also, honor certainly played a role in the youth-led organizations of European academia. Organizations such as the Prussian student *Burschenschaft* held members to a rigid social code. Nevertheless, student organizations and rebellions in Europe differed greatly from those in the southern U.S. colleges, because they were almost universally more politicized. European student actions against authority figures centered on the major political and social changes taking place in their society in the nineteenth century. By mid-century, European states had experienced a rapid transition from feudalistic to industrial societies, causing great upheavals that spurred student action. The tumult of Europe from the time of Napoleon, through the conservative regimes that followed, culminating dramatically in the Revolutions of 1848 forced students to become politically active. Student organizations formed in violation of the laws, student leaders committed political assassinations, and student military groups launched revolution.[14]

Southern students, by contrast, led relatively uneventful lives. The southern United States had not undergone any radical industrial transformation, nor had it sustained any significant period of warfare or political upheaval in the first half of the nineteenth century. The South remained the predominantly agricultural, class-based society it had been in the previous century. Major political and social issues that entertained the consciousness of southern students were tame by comparison to those affecting the lives of European students. The War of 1812, the "Era of Good Feelings," the killing of the national bank, the war with Mexico, and even the growing agitation over the issue of slavery did little more than hone the rhetorical skills of southern students. Only when civil war raised its head did they respond with actions that mirrored their European counterparts' zeal from the previous half century.

Student rebellions and riots make for high drama and are fascinating to study, but another issue that has been overlooked in previous studies is the role of honor in shaping antebellum southern college culture *beyond* the issues of rebelliousness and violence. College students in the Old South were, literally, bound by the code of honor. It provided the basic rules of engagement in all parts of their social and intellectual interaction. It would be too simplistic, however, to say that honor always had a causal effect in these interactions. After all, we cannot forget that these students were still moving from childhood to adulthood. Adolescent immaturity drove many of their actions as well. Nevertheless, the honor ethic was always there, forever tapping on the students' shoulders to remind them of the accepted paths toward leadership and respect in southern society.

"College students" in this study refers to males. Higher education for women in the South certainly existed, but on a much smaller scale than for young men. Indeed, the antebellum period was truly revolutionary in the evolution of female higher education. Little more than finishing schools at the beginning of the nineteenth century, by the time of the Civil War many southern women's seminaries and colleges had developed academic curricula and were providing an education equal to that of male institutions. Nevertheless, according to historian Christie Anne Farnham, "the reality of southern educational institutions for women was the organization of all aspects of the educational experience around the goal of producing an exalted notion of womanhood."[15] Although young female scholars developed adolescent relationships that helped guide their behavior and actions, they were far less influenced by the southern code of honor than male students. For young women, the goal was to conform to the ideal of the southern belle, not to promote the broader societal ethic required of young men. Their collegiate existence was far more proscribed than their male counterparts' by the paternal nature of their institutions of higher learning.[16]

The main sources upon which this study rests are the private correspondence and diaries of southern college students and faculty. These sources are bolstered by published memoirs and reminiscences, as well as minutes from college faculty and board meetings throughout the period. I have quoted from these primary accounts and, for the most part, have kept the nineteenth-century spelling, rather than distract the reader with *sic* or other means of correction. I have also used as many published histories of individual colleges as possible to provide further insights; unfortunately, many of these neglect much description of student life in favor of covering broad institutional changes and development. By necessity, not all seminaries, colleges, and universities that existed in the South are represented in this study, but there is broad regional representation. I have used sources from most southern states, with the hope that I could depict the patterns of student life with a certain degree of accuracy. These sources have confirmed the importance of honor and adolescent attitudes in the college student of the Old South. So, with this structure in mind, let me introduce you to the world of Andrew McCollam and his fellow antebellum southern college students.

CHAPTER I

It's All Academic

FACULTY, CURRICULUM, CHEATING,

AND COMMENCEMENT

A N ASSESSMENT of college students: "They attend classes but make no effort to learn anything"; "They frequently learn what they would better ignore"; "On obscure points they depend upon their own judgment . . . so they become masters of error." Historians have generally agreed with these characterizations when describing college life in the Old South. They have depicted southern college students as mere fops, more concerned with power and position than academic matters. Scholars point to the Draconian rules and regulations, the Puritanical middle-class professors, and the recitation method of learning as key factors in establishing an antagonistic environment in southern institutions of higher learning. According to this view, college students had few academic goals and spent more time at college perfecting their upper-class pretensions in society than in obtaining an education. The problem with these criticisms is that they can be almost universally applied to adolescent scholars of any era. In fact, the quotes at the beginning of this paragraph come from fourteenth-century French critic Alvarus Pelagius.[1]

The rules of honor, combined with natural adolescent development, ensured that the academic world of southern colleges and universities was not ideal. Society dictated that southern students wear their public masks, and this fact influenced students to behave in ways that disturbed adults. When you throw adolescence into the mix, student behavior was even more questionable to those in authority. On the other side of the argument, however, is the fact that the code of honor was what made these students set and achieve academic goals. It made them express pride in their institutions. It urged them to respond to the demands of faculty, the curriculum, and teaching methods. And finally, honor played an important role in placing value on graduation as a mark of accomplishment.

Students generally viewed a college education as an important component in their preparations for careers and their transition into adulthood. Higher education was not necessary to succeed in most antebellum professions, but those who attended college did so because they believed it was important. B. C. Lee, who attended the East Alabama Male College (later Auburn University), expressed the importance of education when he learned that many of his friends from home were going to Mobile, Alabama, to attend medical lectures and become physicians. They could do this without first attending college, which he considered a bad idea. He wrote to his mother: "Nearly all the young men around Autaugaville are making Doctors of themselves; & the majority of them, when they graduate will not be competent to wait on a sick horse. They are not competent to read medicine, as it should be read. I think they should first prepare themselves, acquire an education, & then engage in a profession if they would be successful. Any 'goose' or 'fop,'" he continued, "can study 'at' a profession; but it takes a man who is qualified, to succeed. For that reason I am seeking an education, to fit & qualify myself, for future usefulness, & future influence." He concluded: "Then, if I should take a profession I would certainly be more likely to succeed. 'Victory is won only by those who are prepared for the conflict.'"[2]

This idea that a college education was essential for success came from many quarters. One of the strongest sources was from educated family members, and it is of little surprise that they would often appeal to a student's honor, self-worth, and place in society as arguments in favor of his taking his studies seriously. For instance, John Little had made poor grades at the University of Alabama, but his brother, George Little, a professor of natural philosophy at Oakland College in Mississippi, used his connections to have John dismissed rather than expelled from the university. George then chastised John, writing to him that other family members thought "that it is best to 'let well enough alone' & if you make a good clerk & *behave* yourself, it is all that they desire. . . . I want you, however, to have a *good education* & will do all in my power to assist you (so would they all if you would study)." He continued the pressure by informing John that he had caused his family to shed tears because of his scholastic performance. George wrote that if John had seen those tears, he "would have repented of having done anything to hurt the feelings of such tender & loving friends." In essence, George was telling his brother that his poor performance and lack of ambition had brought shame to his family, a grievous breach of the honor ethic. But George resorted to this level of pressure because of a deeply held belief in the growing importance of a college education. He wrote: "Don't give up the idea of graduating, for I can tell you that I am more & more convinced every day of the absolute necessity of it in the men of your time. Men have hitherto & do still succeed well without it but by the time you are grown things will have changed. The mind is the measure of the man." The advice paid off and John went to Oakland College, where he ultimately graduated, preserving the family name.[3] Similar attitudes about the importance of education for success, both in life and as an honorable gentleman, were shared by a growing number of college students throughout the antebellum South.

These attitudes carried over into the students' feelings about their colleges and universities. Most students maintained a level of pride about their institutions. Their self-concept and public mask demanded that they find the positives of college life. To attend a second-rate institution would bring shame and, therefore, dishonor. Not all southern colleges, however, were the same. There were two general types of institutions of higher learning for men in the Old South—state universities (which included military institutes) and church colleges. Generally, state universities, created by legislators who believed that higher education was important to develop leaders in society, held the most prestige among southern institutions of higher learning. Sectarian colleges, the number of which exploded after 1820, provided good alternatives to the universities. Between 1820 and 1860, more than twenty-five church colleges were founded in the South. Many denominations joined this trend, not only to train ministers, but also because they saw education as an important function of the church. They believed that they could have influence, especially through creating less expensive alternatives to the state universities.[4] This sentiment was well expressed by John B.

Davis, president of the Virginia Collegiate Institute (later Roanoke College), when he wrote for financial support from the Virginia Synod of the Lutheran Church in 1847: "It behooves us to take up the subject of education, and urge it upon the attention of our people. The State, to her dishonor be it said, will not do it; let the church take it in hand, and so far as its influence goes, or its interests are concerned, it will be found, if not a direct and speedy, a certain means of remedying this God-dishonoring and soul-destroying evil."[5] Despite the differing philosophies of their founding, both state and church institutions of higher learning generated intense support and pride from their student bodies.

Students at state universities tended to extol the quality of their academic preparation, and dream about the leadership positions they would obtain as a result of their attendance. James Lee Jr., for instance, was proud to be attending the University of North Carolina. He bragged about it with great vigor. He asserted that the university boasted "a greater number of prominent men than any institution in the United States." As another example of how fine an institution he was attending, Lee told the story of a student transferring to the University of North Carolina from Cambridge for reasons of health. Lee asserted: "He left the Junior class there and was compelled to make up some studies before he could enter here." The only thing that young Lee disliked about the place was the surrounding land. He described it as "the poorest land in creation." He wrote: "The vicinity is so poor that when a man dies they are compelled to *manure* his grave to enable him to rise in the judgement day."[6] Of the University of Virginia, another student wrote in 1856: "I think the Academics Department of this College is the best in the United States. I am very much pleased with their way of teaching. The Proffs think they will have six hundred students this session, there is over five hundred here now, And more new students than was ever before."[7]

The pride echoed in these and similar statements also reflected the fact that state university students had grand aspirations. They saw their education as the path to leadership, fame, and fortune. The letter of a University of North Carolina student to his brother on March 4, 1852, best reflects these sentiments. In it he wrote, "It has just occurred to me that on this day [March 4, Inauguration Day] some infinite time hence

I may be inaugurated President of the United States & I immediately determined to . . . make you happy by promising some lucrative clerkship in Washington at that time, so don't let your natural modesty put you out of mind of my promise when that event shall take place."[8]

The academic reputation at many state institutions created envy and defensiveness in some students attending church colleges. Some left to attend the state school; others remained loyal to the church college, arguing that the quality of education was the same. Trying to discern the reality of which type of institution provided a better education misses the point. Whether a student chose to leave one institution for another—or to remain at an institution and defend it—related, in part, to how that decision would make the student appear. But students who operated within the system of honor also understood that they had some control over this status. Staying at an inferior school only brought shame and dishonor, for instance, if the student *admitted* that it was inferior.

Honor dictated that students put the best possible face on the quality of their education—at least to the outside world. Robert Philip Howell, who attended Trinity College (later Duke University) in 1854 wanted to leave, and he ultimately did so with a flair and dignity that sustained his public persona. When he made his decision, he asked his guardian, Edmund Coor, for money to get home. Coor cut a fifty-dollar bank note in half, sending one piece to Howell, and the other piece to Dr. Braxton Craven, Trinity's president. Coor wanted Craven to make another effort to convince Howell to stay. But when Howell still insisted on leaving, the president refused to give him the other half of the note. Howell later remembered that he then gave Craven his half, "remarking that [Craven's] school was poor and needed the money and I could walk home." Howell then further jabbed that when he was "*prepared* for a 'college' I was going to the University [of North Carolina]." Convinced there was nothing more he could do, Craven finally relinquished the money to Howell, but he included the sullen warning that if Howell went to Chapel Hill, it would be his "ruin." To the contrary, Howell eventually graduated from the University of North Carolina in 1860.[9]

Another example comes from Virginia's Randolph-Macon College, a Methodist institution. Robert Cutler wrote to his father that he could not study there "with the diligence & industry without which no man can arrive to eminence in any profession or science." He explained: "I have become a disciple of the most to be abhorred disease, melancholy. . . . Moreover [the] Southern climate does not suit me. It deprives me of flesh & money." He then proposed that he go to a northern college. He was careful in his argument to his Virginia father, writing, "although I do not wish to imbibe northern principles or to become a subject of sectional prejudices, Yet I greatly prefer an education at the North." It appears that his father did not let him go. He was still a student at Randolph-Macon the next session, and not another word was mentioned about leaving.[10]

Most students who went to church colleges not only remained in place, but expressed positive enthusiasm about their educational opportunities. Honor dictated that these students portray their colleges in the best possible light. They demanded familial approval and societal acceptance that their colleges were solid institutions of higher learning. An example of this type of representation is seen in an 1836 letter from Robert Dabney, a student at the Presbyterian Hampden-Sidney College of Virginia, to his mother. "The new man [a chemistry professor] delivered an introductory address to the students on teusday," he wrote, "which was so good, that they have resolved to request a coppy of him for publication. As soon as I can, I will send you a copy." His ardent hope with this news, however, was that his brother, who had attended the University of Virginia, would have a greater respect for Hampden-Sidney. He concluded the letter: "I hope that when Brother sees it [the address], he will not think so meanly of this college."[11]

Dabney's positive depiction of a faculty member was just one of many responses that southern students had in reaction to the college environment. Faculty authoritarianism, challenging curricula, and teaching methodology all represented threats to student honor. Each of these areas carried the real possibility of embarrassing, or unmasking, a student in front of his classmates. These adolescents, therefore, developed a range of responses to these potential threats to honor, including everything from buckling down and studying harder if they believed they could conquer the situation, to creating havoc as peer groups in the classroom or around the college grounds.

Many historians have asserted that southern students, the sons of the gentry, believed themselves to be socially superior to college and university faculty. There is no doubt that some "classism" took place, but the code of honor, rather than social status, was more responsible for how a student treated a faculty member. Students clearly spent a considerable amount of time ridiculing professors. E. Merton Coulter explained that this behavior came from the students' belief "that the professors were the chief obstacle to their thorough enjoyment of life."[12] The more complex explanation, however, is that these students, who indeed did not want interference with their "enjoyment of life," also lived under the constant threat that these professors might bring them public shame in front of their peers. The very fact that students saw faculty as people who could challenge their honor meant that they considered their professors social equals. Men of a lower social status did not have the power to challenge a southern gentleman's honor. Therefore, students developed a dual relationship with their professors. They respected faculty erudition and the knowledge they could impart and saw them as fellow gentlemen, but they also resented the potential unmasking that faculty power represented.[13]

Student ridicule of professors took many forms. When a student believed himself to be evaluated unfairly in the classroom, he would often defend himself (and his honor) by attacking the abilities or the character of the professor. These attacks usually did not come in the form of open confrontation, for that might lead to further humiliation. Instead, they were done through discussions with other students or through letters to home. When James Mercer Garnett Jr. attended St. Mary's College in Baltimore, Maryland, in 1811, he had tremendous difficulties with his studies. He carefully explained the source of these problems to his parents, asserting that his fellow classmates were "disorderly," making it impossible to study or even to hear the professors. He further argued that the faculty "are universally thought incapable of teaching what they profess."[14] It was a point of honor that the cause of his weaknesses lay not within himself, but with those around him, including the faculty. When University of North Carolina student J. D. Tatum learned that school officials had sent a report to his parents stating that his scholarship was declining, he quickly wrote them, explaining that the cause of the drop was that "one or two of the faculty have taken a dislike to me."

He further argued his case that it was a fault in the faculty character, rather than his own admitted failure to pay attention in recitations. He charged that one of the professors "to whom I recite the Bible lesson this session is a trifling freesoiler and is not respected by any of the students."[15] Using a similar charge to explain to his Georgia parents that he probably would not graduate in his Moral Philosophy course, University of Virginia student Edward Anderson described the professor as "an Ohio man" who had "brought some of his Yankee notions with him."[16]

Potential humiliation also came when professors asserted their roles as disciplinarians. Adolescent college men engaged in a variety of boyhood mischief, and when a faculty member would try to put a stop to it, shame, embarrassment, and dishonor for the students were always possible outcomes. When a new professor from England arrived at the University of Virginia in 1841, students received him "with an illumination, and other demonstrations of respect, such as burning tar barrels, yelling, and other such like dignified and manly proceedings." One student observer pointed out, however, that the students may have had ulterior motives. He wrote, "But perhaps, if he knew how much of this to set down to the students love of frolic, and how much to their good will to *him*, his gratulations to himself might be somewhat diminished. They will probably give him a little insight into this matter, by storming his house, the first time he crosses their sovereign wills, which will be very soon, if he does his duty."[17]

Because all students shared the danger of being unmasked by the faculty in almost any setting, mockery and derision of the faculty became a favorite sport. This is not to say that the students and faculty were openly at war. In fact, the more subtle or clever a student could be in his mockery of a faculty member, the more esteemed he was in the eyes of his classmates. Also, these attacks did not mean that the students disliked or disrespected the faculty member; even popular professors received them. For instance, Maj. Thomas J. Jackson was a favorite professor at the Virginia Military Institute. Although he later wore the nickname "Stonewall," his students chose to label him "Square Box" because of his large feet. Of course, they only called him this behind his back, but more public ridicule also befell this professor, who was known to be overly serious. One student asked Jackson in class if a gun could be constructed that could fire around corners. Jackson believed the question had been asked in earnest, and he informed the student that he would have to take the question under consideration. The next day, the major reported to the class "that in his measured opinion no gun could be manufactured with the capacity of shooting around a corner." The student politely bowed to his professor, Jackson saluted the student, and the boy returned to his seat "with a sickly grin," while the rest of the class tried to maintain its composure.[18] The student who was able to pull off such a public demonstration against his professor was playing within the rules of honor. He had shown the world (at least the world of his classmates—the only world that mattered at the time) that he was clever and the professor, who held the power, could not expose him. If a student could maintain respectability, then he usually maintained respect (although sometimes grudgingly) for the faculty. In 1837, for instance, a Hampden-Sidney student proposed a series of toasts to the faculty at an Independence Day celebration. The first was, "Mr. Powers, Professor of mathematics, may his character prove as impervious to the shafts of Calumny, as the Differential Calculus is to the minds of the Junior Class." His second toast was to the entire faculty, whom one student had described as "pigmies." He offered: "The size is not important if the head and heart is right, as is exemplified by the present members of the Faculty."[19] The tongue-in-cheek nature of these toasts demonstrated a level of admiration and respect for the faculty, while also maintaining the air of a respectable man of honor.

Beyond the faculty, the college curriculum also presented a world of threats to a student's honor. The academic requirements and curriculum of southern colleges and universities did not differ too much from each other or from the accepted practices at universities throughout the country in the antebellum period. All curricula were based, in part, on the medieval concept of the liberal arts, which came from the idea that there were certain studies fitting to a "free" man of distinction. "The seven liberal arts were subdivided in the 'three' (*trivium*) of grammar, rhetoric, and dialectic, and the 'four' (*quadrivium*) of arithmetic, geometry, astronomy, and music."[20] As higher education advanced into the nineteenth century, however, colleges and universities transformed many basic elements of the *trivium* and *quadrivium*. They started offering courses in the natural sciences, with emphases on chemistry and Newtonian physics. More advanced mathematics also emerged, as did the study of modern languages. Most colleges also developed a course in "Moral Philosophy," which sought to create a guide to human behavior through reason and observation, instead of relying solely on divine law.[21] But whereas the study of Latin and Greek started to disappear in northern colleges, southern institutions held on to these disciplines with great fervor, because the classical societies they represented not only helped justify slavery, but also the southern honor ethic.[22]

A solid preparatory education was assumed for southern college students. For admission into most southern colleges and universities, they had to know the fundamentals of both Latin and Greek, and had to be proficient in algebra, geometry, and trigonometry. Because of the varying quality of preparatory education in the United States, most institutions required oral entrance examinations for matriculation. David Wyatt Aiken described in great detail his entrance examination into South Carolina College. He wrote: "We were first examined by Prof Twiss, the Mathematical Sage. He required me to solve a question in Algebra, which I did easily, and then gave me the eleventh proposition, 4th Book Davies Geometry to Demonstrate. Which task was quite as easily performed. Not willing that I should be dismissed with such flying colors, he proposed, 'Mr. Aiken what's the difference between equivalent and equal?' A little hesitating, some stammering, and a confident air carried me through with my definition successfully." Aiken was next examined on "Horaces Ode to Amphion, which I read metrically, translated and parsed so fluently that I was soon dismissed with a compliment." Although he clearly had studied the basics of Latin, he did not have the same preparation in Greek. When asked to read from Xenophon's *Anabasis,* he was unable to do so, explaining "Greek *was* Greek to me." Nevertheless, he "opened and stammered through the required lines about as a two year old child would lisp out its vernacular tongue, listened to his beautiful translation of the passage, and nodded assent to his interrogatory suggestions concerning each word that he parsed, for I knew nothing about parsing Greek." Aiken received mercy from his examiner in this case, however, explaining that the professor had known several of his older brothers and that "no peculiar talent for Greek was latent in my cranium." The last part of the exam consisted of "a few questions in Modern Geography and Ancient History, which were all partially answered." In the end, Aiken "was admitted as I claimed, into the 'Sophomore Standing' class, was allowed two months vacation, and ordered to report again on the first Monday in December."[23]

Upon matriculation into southern colleges and universities, students then faced challenging curricula and teaching methodologies. Recitation was the predominant method of teaching in antebellum southern institutions. With this method, the instructor would assign a long segment of a book (too long to be simply memorized); then, students had to demonstrate knowledge of each sentence, in the correct order of its appearance.[24] Some professors lectured and expected students to take notes. Many of these professors then quizzed the students at the end of the class period to see how much they had absorbed. Examinations came both during and at the end of a session, and their results were public knowledge. In addition, most southern colleges emphasized oration as part of the curriculum, requiring students to prepare speeches on a variety of subjects to be delivered publicly.

The primary motivator in all of these teaching methods was shame. Randolph-Macon College provides the perfect example. There, the method of examination was for all students to be tested orally by *all* faculty at the end of the twenty-week session. The students were then ranked within the top, middle, and bottom thirds of the class. Students ranked in the bottom third had notations of "sustained" or "not sustained" by their names. "Not sustained" meant failure, but the student did not repeat the class; he simply moved on in the program, as there was no mechanism for academic expulsion at Randolph-Macon. Southern colleges such as Randolph-Macon had small enrollments, and they remained afloat from tuition, not endowments. Expelling students could threaten the economic stability of the institutions. With this system, therefore, a student who "failed" every course could graduate, but this never happened because the shame associated with being publicly branded "not sustained" forced poorly performing students to withdraw from the college.[25]

Both the curriculum and teaching methodologies, therefore, presented direct academic challenges to students, but more importantly, they exposed them to possible public humiliation. Failure to master the curriculum could not be hidden from other students in the close-knit communities of southern colleges and universities. In addition, all major teaching methodologies required students to perform publicly on a regular basis. Recitation, oration, and public examinations all held within them the potential for glory or for shame. For these privileged students, failure did not mean that they would never have a career, as it might represent to students of a more modern age. Failure meant that their reputations as men of honor might come into question. These young, inexperienced men, therefore, chose to react to this overwhelming pressure in a variety of ways. Some studied, determined to master the curriculum through hard work. Others cheated, determined to make it appear that they had mastered the curriculum. Still others rebelled in more serious and direct ways, or carried out pranks, to make it appear that they did not take academe seriously—a personal choice not to study and get marks, instead of an inability to do so. The variety of methods chosen reflected the lack of maturity among college students. Mere boys when they arrived at college, southern students struggled to define their identities as men of honor, but they could not let the curriculum or the classroom get in their way.

Many students chose to rise to their academic challenges through hard work, although even that did not always guarantee success. Robert Dabney of Hampden-Sidney wrote to his brother that he was preparing for an examination. He explained: "To a good student, the time devoted to reviewing his studies is the easiest, but that is not exactly my case. I have determined that study and attention shal not be wanting. It is so generally the case that a young mans character is determined the first session he is at college, that if you do not bear a good one at your first examination, the Professors will be prepossessed against you forever afterwards. It is therefore doubly important to study well this session."[26] When hard work paid off, students felt exhilaration at their success, and, no doubt, at their ability to thwart humiliation through their mental prowess. William S. Mullins, of the University of North Carolina, wrote in his diary that his class had begun studying calculus. In the evening he worked for two hours to solve eight problems given by the professor. He exclaimed that "never have [I] commanded my attention steadily on a single subject for so long a time before . . . and I have seldom felt better than when at nine oclock, I laid down the book after having solved all the questions." His victory, however, was not shared by all of his classmates. He explained that many in the class "cannot solve a problem in quadratics unassisted, and of course to these, Calculus, is a redoubtable monster: and their curses, complaints, and fears are expressed in all the various and forcible forms contained in the comprehensive vocabulary of College slang."[27]

Innovative teaching methods occasionally appeared, but met mixed reviews from the students. A Hampden-Sidney student reported favorably about an experiment on a cat performed by his chemistry professor in 1834. "He was lecturing on anatomy, and had a large cat brought in and by dropping about two drops of poison of some sort on the animals tongue, killed it in less than a minute. He said that this poison was weak, having been kept some time, and that when he first tried it it killed a cat quicker than if he had cut off his head. He then caused the dead cat to move and jerk in various ways, and even to sneeze, by applying electricity to her nerves."[28] Not every innovation, however, met with approval from the students. In 1860, Virginia's Roanoke College president, Daniel Bittle, took a class on a "geological expedition to the top of a mountain about twenty miles from the college." The students, however, were not impressed by the trip because it rained the entire time. In fact, their analysis of this "hands-on curriculum" even had a more practical complaint. "We all voted it a bone," wrote one student to his mother about the trip, "to have to hire horses and ride forty miles to see a few rocks when there are plenty of the same kind in the cabinet."[29]

Choosing study and hard work as their response to academics became more than some students could handle. In 1840 one student had to withdraw because of a severe case of dyspepsia (indigestion). The cause seems to have been the stress of the college curriculum. One of his friends wrote that the "hard study he underwent last session" brought on the ailment, further explaining that the young man had felt better after a summer's vacation, but only one week into a new term, his dyspepsia returned.[30] Another student at the University of North Carolina had been admitted on probation and was determined to make up his deficiencies quickly. He studied every night until 2:00 A.M., and then rose at 4:30 A.M. to go to prayers. After two weeks of this schedule, the student became seriously ill, unable to hold down food or water. He later reported that he had decided to "cease studying and from that time I commenced improving."[31]

Even when students were resolute in their efforts to meet the academic challenges facing them, they still risked breaching the code of honor. James Gwyn, a student at Emory and Henry College in Virginia, had to give a speech to the student body as one of his academic requirements. He chose as his topic "The State of North Carolina." When he delivered it, the students from North Carolina gave "wonderful and uncommon cheering." Even though Gwyn had won the hearts of the North Carolinians, he found he had alienated many of the Tennesseans. Of them, he wrote, "We have been very intimate, but now seem distant." Although he claimed he intended no insult, he did minimize the importance of something the Tennesseans held dear: their beautiful mountain scenery. Gwyn had not wanted to discuss the mountain scenery of North Carolina in his speech. As a method of avoiding the subject, therefore, he stated that some admired their mountain scenery, and then he dismissed this by "merely" remarking "that Patagonia could do that." The entire student body talked of nothing but the "insult," and regional rivalries erupted. This excitement continued for two weeks before other events took attention away from it.[32] The lesson Gwyn learned, however, was that within the tightly constructed world of honor, words matter. Insults, no matter how small, were seen as challenges.

Hard-working students also recognized the importance of associating with others with the same determination to excel through studious habits. Robert Dabney of Hampden-Sidney asserted that it was common for students to help each other out with their studies. He ascribed to the students "a most perfect spirit of generosity in all such things as the loan of books and assistance in each others studies. All our things are regarded pretty much as a common stock, amongst intimate acquaintances and neighbours." Nevertheless, Dabney also expressed concern about his roommate's study habits in a letter to his mother. He wrote: "My room mate is a very good sort of young man, and . . . I think we shal agree very well. He seems very anxious to study, but does not stay much in his own room. This is a bad symptom, for however it may be in other matters he who gads about does not study. It is very important for a student to make himself well acquainted with his own room."[33] Similarly, in 1834 a University of North Carolina student wrote to his father about his roommate: "For the first two months he made no noise, studied hard, and behaved himself well and properly and I liked him very much, the affection was reciprocated, but after a while he got a fiddle and of course got among the fiddlers in college [who are] idle and worthless fellows. . . . He began to drink considerably and to have wines and brandy continually, and a boy of about 15, I am afraid he will not do much good in this world."[34] Another University of North Carolina student agreed that one's associations made a difference in whether study was the course he chose. In reflecting on his first experience at college, he asserted that when he arrived, he had no roommates, so he began associating with the young men living closest to him. These friends, he would later write, were "the three most dissipated students in College." He said that with their influence he became a "rowdy." He explained: "I was drunk almost every night and kept liquor habitually in my room, and created a general disturbance in the building." After his first term, he realized that these activities had hurt him, so he changed his patterns and associations and became quite studious.[35]

Reacting to the curriculum and teaching methods with study was also difficult because of distractions. In some cases the college location offered too many distractions for students. Dabney at Hampden-Sidney described his college as follows: "This place is not remarkable for anything atall except poverty for the college stands in the middle of an old field full of gullies and weeds and the cows of the neighbourhood come up to the very windows with their bells, making such a noise that I can not study."[36] Another distraction was other students, because although some students chose to apply themselves to their studies, many others did not, and these "rowdy" students often made things difficult for the more studious scholars. Hector James McNeill, a student at the University of North Carolina, wrote that upon arriving at the college he was going to have to make up some studies to catch up with his class. He then asserted: "I am not very well satisfied—being a little behind my class I shall have to study very hard & close all the time—and there is the greatest amount of profanity used certainly of any other place & upon the whole it is a very dissipated place." Despite the difficulties these distractions posed for him, he also added: "The longer I stay the better I like it."[37] James Garnett's experience at St. Mary's College in Baltimore was not so agreeable. He explained to his parents that "the boys are so noisy in c[l]ass and so disorderly in the study room, that I can not study well or even hear the explanations which the masters give in the classes."[38]

The disorderly behavior described by Garnett represented a second major way in which students reacted to the challenges of the curriculum and teaching methods. The rebelliousness of students against the faculty showed the power struggle that developed between the two groups. This struggle, however, was not simply a case of elitist, slave-owning students refusing to submit to their socially inferior professors' wills, as some historians have asserted; instead it was the immature reaction of adolescents defending themselves against potential threats to their public face. John Henry wrote that at the University of Virginia the "fellows make more noise than any place I ever was at. . . . In the classroom sometimes if the professor says anything out of the way, they will stamp about fifteen minutes. they all make it a rule to run every new teacher that comes here."[39] The students at the University of North Carolina were having a tough time with a mathematics book, Pierce's *Mathematics in the United States*. For years, students had complained about the difficulty of this book. In 1851 a rumor started floating around that the book was no longer being printed and that copies were impossible to find. In November, the students took drastic action: they collected the seventy or eighty copies of the book found on the campus, piled them into a stack, and created a huge bonfire of them. The plan worked. The faculty placed those students who had been studying calculus from the book into an astronomy class and those studying analytics into philosophy.[40] In essence, these students had perceived a threat to their honor in the possibility of humiliation and shame brought on by the difficult curriculum, so they lashed out and preserved their honor by destroying the source of their anguish.

In addition to studying hard or open defiance, southern college students also chose a third reaction to the curriculum and teaching methods—cheating. It seems incongruous to discuss cheating as a method of preserving honor, but for many, that was exactly what it represented. When faced with the possibility of humiliation, the southern code recognized that saving face was more important than conforming to moral or ethical rules of behavior. In at least one instance this practice was even endorsed by a student's parent. When William Mullins's father learned that his son was to deliver an address before the University of North Carolina, he told a friend that he wanted the boy to deliver an article published in the *London Metropolitan* as his speech. He said that if his son used the article as his own, that no one would be the wiser and he would "have the praise of the world to an uncommon degree showered upon" his head. When the friend tried to reason with the father that this course would be inappropriate, the father responded that "Plagiarism in preference to Dunceyism" was his motto.[41]

At the University of North Carolina, a philosophy professor's rigidity aided his students in their dubious preparations. In 1849, Thomas Miles Garrett wrote in his diary that he had "commented very thoroughly" when called upon to recite that day in the class. He wrote: "I was called upon as I expected and made a pretty good recitation. I am now free for three or four lessons." But how did he know he would be singled out that day, or that he would not be called upon again for three or four days? He explained: "The class is so large that each student does not recite but about every fourth time and the Professor is so regular that we can always tell when we are going to be called on to recite."[42]

Cheating became a serious problem at many other institutions, both large and small, throughout the South. At St. Mary's College in Baltimore, James M. Garnett wrote that "in classes here where they commit to memory almost every one hide their books behind their desks and say their lessons out of them, & in some of the classes that I am in, every one does it but my self."[43] At larger institutions the problem was just as bad. By 1859 cheating at the University of Mississippi "reached phenomenal proportions." Many of the examinations taken at the university came in a standard format published by a firm in Philadelphia. Some students went so far as to hire agents in Philadelphia to inform them of the approximate arrival date of the questions in Oxford; then the students stole the questions when they arrived.[44] Similarly, cheating had become so extensive at the University of Alabama that the institution had to pass several new rules in 1848 to deal with the problem. For instance, students entering recitation rooms had to put their books and all notes away from their seats. When a student was called to recite, he had to move to a vacant space away from his seat. Students called to the blackboard were not allowed to wear a cloak. The new rules even said that if a student held a position or posture that could raise suspicion, the professor could give him a mark of "o" for the day's recitation, whether the student was to be called to recite that day or not.[45]

Cheating, disruptions in the classroom, challenges to the professor, and even studying hard all represented the panoply of responses used by students to cope with the potential humiliation represented by the faculty, the curriculum, and the teaching methods. Southern honor did not cause these reactions, but it did weigh heavily in the background. Despite the imperfect nature of southern higher education, however, students did learn, and when they graduated they took with them their pride. Because of their tenacious adherence to the code, therefore, one of the most important components of their college careers was commencement.

At every southern college and university, commencement exercises took on great significance. The students, who had arrived as mere boys, were now moving into the world as leaders of their society. It was a rite of passage like no other in the antebellum South. Commencements were attended by a cross-section of southern society—politicians, planters, small farmers, businessmen, and even slaves. Students stood public examinations, gave speeches, staged debates and plays, and received their degrees. Often, commencement exercises took on a carnival atmosphere.[46] Maryville College graduate W. E. Caldwell reflected on his commencement: "By the end of the session, September, 1848, I had completed the College course of study. . . . Graduation day was a grand day to me and, of course to all the class. We all passed a creditable examination, and got through our orations with success. But, the glory of the occasion did, from the ending as from the beginning of our course, [show] how distance lends enchantment to the view."[47]

Commencement exercises, filled with grandeur, clearly generated pride in the students. William H. Burwell, a student at the University of North Carolina, wrote to his father in 1855: "We received our regalia and clothes from Philadilphia the other [day]. I think my clothes fit very well and the Regalia is the pretyest I ever saw but it is made for the rong side. it is made for the right instead of the left as it should be, but I think we can have it altered here." These fineries, however, did not come cheaply. Burwell further admitted that "my Bill was sent with my clothes which was $100. dollars. please send me 40. dollars if it is convenient as I wish to pay for my regalia now and several more little things. I hope that you will not think that I am extravagant. I have been chosen one of the Marshals and dont wish to be called close and I know you will indulge me for the preasant."[48] Other expenses for the ceremonies often included new clothes, gifts, and money for the variety of celebrations connected to the commencement. William Whitfield even asserted that a dancing master came to the University of North Carolina every year in the spring "to give the students dancing lessons preparatory to commencement."[49]

The nature of the commencement exercises gave students the opportunity to step forward into the public eye as men of intellect. Speeches occupied the largest portion of the exercises. Robert Dabney described the celebrations at Hampden-Sidney to his brother as follows: "There are as you doubtless know two rival societies. From each of these, there is a satirical oration, an english oration upon any general subject, an oration in latin or greek, and a forensic upon some question, of which one side is supported by a member of one society, and the other by a member of the other. The classical orations are spoken in latin by the member of one society, and in greek by the member of the other, alternately." In addition to giving speeches, students performed plays, with one society performing a tragedy and the other a comedy. Dabney's Philanthropic Society was to perform the tragedy that year, which he proclaimed to be "the most difficult task, for it requires a much higher degree of talent to make a tragedy inter[es]ting to a promiscuous audience, than a comedy." He assured his brother that the play would not be boring, however, promising that it would contain "some buffoonery which pleases." Such activities were expensive, but generally considered important. Dabney, however, had to refuse what he called "a very good part" because of his lack of funds. He explained: "The actors have to buy their own dresses, and they are necessarily quite expensive." Even though he was not personally participating, his enthusiasm reflected the pride generated by the ceremonies. He urged his brother to attend so that he could "see how respectably we perform."[50]

The speeches given at commencement were designed to demonstrate the academic achievements of the honorable graduates. At Centenary College, in Louisiana, a former president remembered that in the early 1850s he had worked the students hard to prepare their speeches. He wrote: "They had written and re-written their pieces; had had them rigidly criticized and thoroughly corrected. They had also practiced them before me and had given much attention to their delivery." On the day of the commencement a large crowd gathered to hear the speeches. After several of the students had performed well, Calvin Hines, one of the brightest seniors, was due to give his oration. According to the president, Hines "had written an address which would have done credit to one more mature than he was. It was full of poetic sentiment, and glowed with the creations of an exuberant imagination." But after a promising start, the student "came to a dead halt, uttering these words: 'Ever and anon.' After a most awkward pause he again repeated 'Ever and anon.' Another halt. (Confusion—disappointment!) Has he forgotten his piece? Again he repeated 'Ever and anon' and again he stopped." At that point someone on the stage motioned for the boy to sit down. Many had sympathy for Hines, but some in the crowd started to hiss. Then, the student "rose almost to tiptoe. He advanced to the very front of the stage, and, in a voice indicating self-possession, energy, determination, triumph, he again repeated, 'Ever and anon, as I look abroad upon the magnificent works of nature; as I behold the sun in his matchless career through the heavens, I see him accompanied to his setting by the most gorgeous clouds, which, like so many chariots of gold and crimson and blue, follow in a triumphal procession; and then when I look up to the mighty heavens and behold the firmament, the work of His fingers, the moon and the stars which He has ordained, I can but exclaim, 'Great and marvelous are thy works; in wisdom hast thou made them all.'" The president characterized the rest of the speech as follows: "On he went; the Rubicon was crossed; his words burned; his thoughts breathed; his language glowed; his voice rang out; his harmonious and often gorgeous sentences, as clear as ever a bell sent forth in answer to its ringing tongue." Hines had created such tension among the people of the audience that, when he finally successfully completed his speech, they erupted into a "deafening shout of applause." He was considered "the hero of the day" because he had "fairly won his spurs, and almost every other speech was forgotten amid the triumphs which young Hines had wrested from defeat itself." The president concluded: "After the exercises were all over there was much discussion as to whether that hero of the hour had been merely acting a part, or whether he had really forgotten his piece. I never knew. I simply give the incident as one of the most remarkable I ever witnessed on a commencement occasion."[51]

Whether the drama of Hines's speech was contrived or not, honor had played a part in the day's ceremony. By going onto the stage, Hines had implicitly assured the audience that he could deliver a speech worthy of a college graduate. If, therefore, he could not deliver such an oration, he was as much as publicly admitting that he was a liar—a grievous breach of the code of honor. The audience, which understood these dynamics all too well, played its part. Some had begun to hiss him, basically stating that they believed him to be dishonorable. Others felt sympathy for him because they knew the gravity of his troubles if he could not pull off this speech. When he finally "rose almost to tiptoe" and finished the poetic oration, he had fulfilled his contract and had proven himself not to be a liar. He was an honorable man.

Not all commencement speeches held such a high degree of drama or were meant to be taken seriously. At the University of North Carolina, just before the commencement ceremony, every senior had to present a speech at the "Senior Speaking." They chose their own topics, which ranged from serious political studies to more general societal and cultural themes. William Whitfield wrote, for instance, that a senior named Strong presented a piece of poetry entitled, "Woman." He said that it "took very well with the ladies, I reckon." Several seniors gave speeches that Whitfield labeled "funnies." These were orations aimed at tickling the audience's sense of humor. He reported: "Barrett's [speech] was the best 'funny' that I ever heard. His subject was 'A new study in our college course' and in speaking he said that the 'new study' was Courtship. He was the last man that spoke and when he got through some of his classmates rode him out on their shoulders. He didn't crack a smile the whole time he was speaking."[52] So, despite the subject matter, Barrett had won acclaim because of his cleverness, and he had succeeded in the public arena as an honorable man should.

Commencement marked the end of the academic struggles in more ways than one. Of course, it held its traditional, official meaning of denoting the completion of the required course of study and the awarding of degrees. But commencement also meant that a different type of struggle had come to an end as well—the fight to maintain honor when it had been continuously assailed by the very academic system that had educated them. Graduates would never again have to be in a situation in which, on such a constant basis, they would be in danger of losing face—of being humiliated before their peers. They would not have to create distractions or overcome as many obstacles in their paths. They were now educated men of the world, but more specifically, honorable men of the South. Indeed, they had a sense that life for them was changing, and that they were going to miss the joys of college life—the friendships, the intellectual environment, and the adventure of being away from home. But what they would not miss was the constant potential of being proven dishonorable. The sense of relief they felt at this stage of their lives coming to an end was well represented by Samuel Lander Jr. in his valedictory speech at Randolph-Macon College's 1852 commencement:

> It also gives us much pleasure to know that we will never again be forced to apply our attention to the uninteresting text-books of a College course. We have been called upon to admire the beautiful manoeuvers of your Phosphuretted Hydrogen struggling into being: We have given up in despair, after having made strenuous endeavors to remember the characteristics of your Asclepiadic Choriambic Tetrameters:—We have perplexed our brains by attempting to comprehend the mysterious non-tangibility of the Asymptotes of the Hyperbola:—We have stood in mute astonishment in contemplation of the alleged simplicity of your ultimate ideas: . . . And shall we, under these circumstances, profess to be almost heart-broken, while shouts of joy would more significantly express our feelings.[53]

Lander and his fellow graduates were leaving the academic world they had entered as boys, and were entering into the world beyond. Their academic training would serve them well as they rose to positions of power on the plantation or in the halls of government. But beyond the oratorical skills and knowledge base they had acquired, they had also been trained in what was expected of them as men of honor. They had earned their stripes on the academic field of battle, and now they could advance as victors of the honor wars.

CHAPTER 2

On Campus

ANTEBELLUM SOUTHERN COLLEGE
STUDENTS AND THEIR ENVIRONMENT

IN JULY 1845, fifteen-year-old John Jacob Scherer, accompanied by his father, left home for the Virginia Collegiate Institute. Before his departure, Jacob's mother gave him "several dollars in little pieces of silver money." After sixty miles of the trip, Jacob's father turned back, severing the last tie to the safety of home and childhood. For Jacob, this journey was a grand adventure, but it did not mean that he would develop into an adult immediately. In fact, shortly after he arrived at the institute, he accidentally broke a glass inkstand and received a severe reprimand. In his own words, his reaction was less than "adult": "I went out behind the building and wept, and longed and longed for mother."[1]

Antebellum southern college students were on a journey throughout their college careers. They searched for growth and respect within the adult world of the Old South. The road on which they traveled, however, was not straight and easy. They met many challenges from their very environment. The way they reacted to this environment reflected how far down the path to adulthood they had gone.

For many, the first difficulties in their journey came on their way to college. In the summer of 1837, for instance, University of North Carolina student T. R. Caldwell stayed the night in Salisbury, North Carolina, on his way to Chapel Hill. In the watch pocket of his waistcoat, Caldwell's father had placed several folded bills to cover expenses. Upon his arrival at Chapel Hill, Caldwell discovered that a thief had replaced the bills with folded paper during his stay at Salisbury.[2]

Other University of North Carolina students faced more hazardous obstructions on their journeys. In 1853, several students hired wagons in Raleigh to take them to Chapel Hill on roads described as "almost impassable." When they got to within eight miles of the university, all of the wagons got mired in the mud. Several walked on that night, or hired the horses to ride. One of the unfortunate travelers, however, had become too ill to continue on, so he and a friend approached the nearest house and asked to stay the night. They gained entrance, but not without initial resistance. According to the ill student, "the old Lady of the house hesitated for a while and said that she had determined not to let any of the students stay there, but she said she 'sposed' she would have to let me stay, so I went to bed immediately and soon entirely recovered, and then got up and dressed and went down and chatted with the old lady a while."[3]

George Penn faced similar travel difficulties during his 1841 trip to Washington College in Virginia. Having planned to travel by stagecoach, Penn was disappointed to find that the route had been discontinued because of poor road conditions. He soon learned, however, that there was a regular mail run to Lexington using a horse cart, so he purchased a berth on the cart. When he finally arrived at college, he complained that the ride had been the most uncomfortable of his life—so much so that he asserted, "every bone in me was either broke or dislocated."[4]

For other students, however, the trip to college brought amusement. Upon arriving at the University of Virginia in 1846, for instance, two Alabama students spent their first night on the outskirts of town in a private home, sharing a room with two other students. After such a long trip, the Alabamians were exhausted and went to bed immediately. They found that they could not go to sleep easily because, as one of the Alabama boys wrote, they were "intently watching one of the other fellows who was walking about the room looking very much disturbed and as if he wished to do something without knowing how to get at it." He continued, "After pacing backwards and forwards two or three times what does the fellow do but come whack down on his *knees* and go to praying! just as if he was not at the University! God! I gave Tom a *pinch* or *two* and we like to have died—as soon as he got up we made some observation and then both *roared out*."[5]

Like these Alabama students, many discovered that the college environment did not always meet their expectations. Many southern colleges were more isolated than some students expected. Augusta College in Kentucky was just such an institution. Virginia youth Robert White-head attended there in 1830, and after a few weeks he wrote: "This place is but a small one right on the banks of the river. Nothing here to cheer one's spirits. It is one of the most lonesome places I ever was at. It is 45 miles from Cincin[a]tti and 18 from Maysville from which place it is 60 miles to Lexington and 45 from there to Stanford."[6]

Attachment to home, and therefore to childhood, can be seen in letters like Whitehead's. Even though he had chosen to cross his adolescent bridge to adulthood at college, his ties to childhood and home remained strong. Students understood this dichotomy. Emory and Henry College student Leonidas Siler demonstrated his awareness of the value of college in his journey to adulthood in an 1846 letter: "I know that my separation from home, is for my own good & on that account, with hard work, I can reconcile my feelings, to my lot." Nevertheless, in the same letter Siler expressed a deep desire to maintain some connection to his childhood. He argued that he could accept his "lot" better "if I could only have one of my old acquaintances with me. But so far, I have been entirely by myself."[7] Other students expressed themselves more directly. "I never wanted to see home so bad in my life," wrote University of North Carolina student William Burwell to his father. "I feel as if I have been up hear six months." Perhaps to convince his father of the worthlessness of college, Burwell added that nothing of interest ever occurred there, "except that we find a good many calves and geese every morning in the recitation room."[8]

Even though young students had these strong emotions tying them to the safety of their homes, the college environment did eventually help mold them into adults. Time was the key. Students who stayed in school, adjusted to their new lives, and started to cut the ties to home found great benefits from their college experiences. A sense of the need to "stick it out" can be seen in the advice of a University of North Carolina student to his younger sister, who was just beginning college herself. "Try to be sociable, make as many friends as possible and get the ill will of no one," wrote F. M. Johnson in 1857. "Dont trouble yourself about home folks too much. I know how much I used to think about home, when if I had been studying my lessons I might have known more." His closing advice, however, reflects the sense that time was what best helped to sever the connection to childhood. He wrote: "I know how you feel[,] you feel just like you was visiting all the time. However this will all soon pass over."[9]

One of the areas of the college environment that made students feel as if they were "visiting all the time" was their accommodations. As sons of the southern gentry, college students had grown to expect decent living quarters, but at college they seldom got them. Not all of the colleges and universities in the South had residential living on the grounds. In fact, most students had to find their own living arrangements in the community around the college. Nevertheless, whether college students lived on the college grounds or in the town, in a dormitory or in a boardinghouse, alone or with a roommate, their housing situation played an important role in the journey toward adulthood.

Often, students had to work hard to find a place to live. In the fall of 1856, Tennessean J. F. Henry arrived at the University of Virginia after the session had begun. A friend had obtained a room for him "outside of the precincts" of the university. Henry wrote: "I was so much displeased with it that I would not have my trunk sent down and went straight away to the University to see if I could not get a better one but found I could not do it." Henry's fortune improved, however, when he was able to find new accommodations at the university the next day. He explained that another acquaintance "had a room on the Eastern Lawn without a companion, and offered me the place, which I accepted with pleasure." He concluded: "I think I was very lucky after being so late to obtain such a good room and desirable companion. He is very much a gentle man, and very studious. Our room is in a very quiet part of the Lawn and I think I can do a good deal of hard studying."[10]

In contrast to Henry's desire to live on the campus, some students found pleasant living circumstances when they resided in private homes. In 1855 William Gibson Field described one such positive experience. He wrote: "About a week before the commencement of the session (Sept. 20), I reached Hampton Sidney College and secured a large comfortable room at 'Rat Castle,' the residence of Professor Hollander." Fields referred to the house as "ancient and honorable" and reported that he lived there with five other students, Professor Hollander, and Professor Halladay. In describing his living situation, he raved, "The residents of Rat Castle possessed enjoyments *unknown* in college. We had good servants to wait on us, good water, and ice in abundance . . . in short, [we] enjoyed all the advantages of college without its annoyances."[11]

Whether on campus or off, students had several responsibilities in setting up their living arrangements. In 1857, Georgian Edward Anderson wrote to his mother about the work he had put into his room: "I have been very busy getting my room ready ever since I got here, & I moved in last night for the first time, with all the pomp and bustle of an army entering a conquered city." He assured her that he had more work to do, but that "with my carpet down & a nice fire blazing in the fire place my room looks quite cozy already."[12] The next year, in a letter to his father, he went into more detail, and the picture was not quite as rosy. He wrote, "You are obliged to furnish your room entirely[,] they do not even supply you with a bed or towels[,] everything has to be bought; they have iron bedsteads and washstands . . . which they sell to the students, charging for the bedstead, mattress, a pillow, bolster, a pair of blankets, a comfort, a coverlid, two pair of sheets, 2 pillow cases, the washstand with pitcher, basin, & everything complete, thirty four dollars." Anderson was not pleased with this obligation, especially after he had paid the university prices, then later discovered he could have purchased the goods elsewhere for much less. The main target of his complaint against the university furnishings was the bed. "I do not like the beds," he lamented, "for in the first place they are too low and every one that comes in the room will be lounging upon them so that they will never be in decent order, but my great objection is that they would fit a man about three inches shorter than myself than they do me."[13]

Other students also complained about their furnishings. James Mercer Garnett of St. Mary's College in Maryland had an experience similar to Anderson's. The bed was "six inches shorter than I am & so narrow that I can scarcely turn over in the night without throwing all the covering off."[14] A more urgent problem for some, however, was not the size of the bed, but the insects that accompanied it. "When I left home," recalled University of North Carolina student N. F. Neal, "I hardly knew what a chinch was but now [I] have become pretty well acquainted with the customers, for I sleep with a good many and by that means have scraped acquaintances. I would have the bed scalded but I suspect that the matress is full . . . so it would do but little good[;] they get on me in the day or anytime I lay down almost."[15] Vermin in the beds were apparently enough of a problem that University of Virginia student George Knox Miller quoted a friend's poem on the topic:

The cursed fleas the cursed feleas [*sic*]—
Have hoppéd forth from their wintry sleep;
And with the most surprising ease,
O'er my poor limbs have 'gun to creep.
Now who can doubt that a *goodthing,*
Always brings along its evils;
Since it is seen that lovely spring,
Hatches out these little *devils.*
They bite; they tickle; and they sting,
The student bending o'er his book;
Till at them, curses, he does fling;
Then ope's his shirt and 'gins to look.
Thus harrasséd he'll soon determine,
To close the labors of the day;
And in the bed, with the vermin,
He snores all night, an easy prey.[16]

College and university housing also subjected students to another variety of pest—other students. In 1840, John Coles Rutherfoord wrote to his father about his difficulties with studying and his appreciation that he lived in a boardinghouse rather than at the college. There, he said, idle students entered rooms, "preventing those who are disposed to be studious from being so." He continued: "They never seem to think of knocking at your door, but in they walk, throw themselves unceremoniously on your bed, and if you do not interfere, they will cut up your books, break your combs, and destroy or deface everything they can lay their hands upon." He also complained about the state of the rooms at the college, stating: "All the rooms I have seen, present the appearance of Dog-kennels—so defaced have they already become with Tobacco juice, mud, water-melon-seed, & &."[17]

University of North Carolina student T. R. Caldwell had a similar attitude about his fellow collegians. In response to his father's inquiry about a roommate, Caldwell wrote, "I am glad to say that I am alone this session for I find it much better to be without a roommate[;] the room is easier kept clean, and I am apt to be less troubled with company."[18] Hampden-Sidney College student John S. Dyerle probably would have preferred Caldwell's arrangement. In 1859, he seemed on the edge of a breakdown trying to deal with his inconsiderate fellow students. He wrote: "I am very much annoyed by some noisy fellows about College who keep a fuss night and day." On his floor he faced particular difficulties—he deemed it "worse than any in College." The students there, he explained, were nothing more than a "pretty *rowdy* crowd" and "fools altogether." The noise that particularly grated on Dyerle, driving him to distraction, came from the young man who occupied the room above him. Dyerle accused the student of having "half sense," because he was "continually dancing or dragging his old trunk or table or throwing his old chairs or bed-stead about." To top off the complaints, the fellow also had "an old flute." Dyerle was desperate. He said that the flute was the last thing he heard when he went to sleep at night, and that "as soon as the old bell taps in the morning at five oclock he bounds out of bed and begins [again]." Dyerle finished his description by claiming that the tormenter from above was even at that moment dancing, which was causing Dyerle's door & window sash to make more noise "than forty threshing machines."[19]

The close nature of student living presented some difficulties more serious than noise. Fire always represented a severe danger to nineteenth-century lives—especially when large numbers of people lived in one building. University of North Carolina student Thomas Miles Garrett described one such fire in the dormitory in 1849. According to Garrett, one of his fellow students "had attempted to replenish his lamp with oil or camphine, without extinguishing the light of it." The result, he wrote, was to be expected because of the "ignitable quality of the fluid." The liquid in both the lamp and the canister "caught fire, and produced a general conflagration." Garrett reported that the student was so stunned that he stood there without attempting to extinguish the flames. Had the flames not been seen from another building, he argued, "the whole building in which were quartered fifty students all wrapt in sleep might have been extinguished." Garrett himself ultimately put out the fire, but he wrote, "It is impossible to conceive how much excitement this produced. Some student of such strong lungs hollered fire! fire! fire! so long and so loud, that the country people caught the alarm." Garrett claimed that their cries were so loud that they "verberated and reverberated among the hills fully some distance around and possibly waked the owles[,] hawks, bears and panthers of the Blue ridge, and it may be that the . . . sound is yet resounding along the shores of the Atlantic and that the wild Arabs of the Eutopous realm have been aroused from their drowsy slumber."[20]

In each of these housing situations, whether life-threatening fires or annoying pests, these adolescents were learning what it was to face the problems associated with close living quarters. They used the experiences they gained and made creative solutions to the problems they faced. One of the other difficulties in housing demonstrates this well. In the winter, students had to worry about keeping warm in the drafty, noninsulated buildings of the day. For some students the solution to this problem came as a simple market transaction. At Hampden-Sidney College, all students had to pay $2.75 per term for firewood. Robert Dabney bragged in 1836 that he and his roommate had two cords piled near their door. He wrote that "the passages are full of wood at present, as the students have just had a large quantity brought in."[21]

Other students, however, found more creative solutions to this problem. In May 1860, Chapel Hill, North Carolina, experienced an unseasonably cold spell. Being late in the term, most students at area boardinghouses had already used up all of their firewood for the year. University student William B. Whitfield and his roommate, however, devised a plan to get their landlady to hand over some of her wood. Whitfield's roommate "moved all the books off the table, pulled off his shoes, picked up a coffee pot . . . and got up on the table and commenced dancing & singing and rattling the coffee pot." The landlady came running to see what all the commotion was about, and the roommate calmly explained that they were dancing to keep warm. The woman immediately told the boys to go to the woodpile and help themselves, which they did.[22]

Another aspect of the college environment linked to so many young men living together was dealing with illness. The manner in which students handled illness so far from home reflected their adolescent ambiguity. With illness, many slipped back into childhood, wanting their mother's care and comfort; others forged ahead, vowing to handle the problem on their own. Either way, illnesses and epidemics played a major role in the college environment and how students reacted to it.

In 1842, students at Washington College experienced "considerable excitement" because a contagious disease they presumed to be smallpox was spreading through Lexington, Virginia, and the surrounding countryside. George Penn, a student at the college, wrote to his mother that if another case of the disease arose in the town, then he and several of his classmates had resolved to leave the area rather than risk catching the illness.[23]

Penn's reactions were reasonable, especially considering the relative isolation of Lexington and the possibility of the disease spreading. In a similar situation, Centenary College in Jackson, Louisiana, found itself without students in 1860 because of fear of contagion. The local physician had gone to a plantation near the college to attend to a slave woman with smallpox. Shortly thereafter, when two members of the doctor's family turned up with the disease, fear spread throughout the college. Every student left within a day, and the college president had to cancel commencement.[24]

Of course, some students used the excuse of escaping disease to try to force a vacation from their studies. "In college one great subject of conversation is the sickness," wrote University of Virginia student Edward Anderson in 1857. Some of his classmates, he continued, hoped to use the excuse of an epidemic "to get off for a few weeks" so they were "trying to raise a panic."[25]

In some cases, however, students took more responsibilities in the face of disease rather than using the threat as an excuse for vacation. In 1860 a diphtheria epidemic struck Roanoke College. One student penned in a letter that he hoped he would not catch it because "it does not look very pleasant at all events." He further explained that if the disease were fully contagious, "the whole of the college will catch it as all have taken their turns in watching by the sick."[26] This example illustrates an important point about college students and their environment:

namely, when there were several students sick, the only people who could care for them were fellow students. Illness forced many to grow up—perhaps before they were ready.

Illness brought to students a sense of their mortality. It coerced students into seeing that life—contrary to their adolescent conceptions—could come to an end quickly. An 1833 cholera epidemic in Kentucky brought this stark reality to students at Augusta College. "It seems as if Kentucky is the 'bloody ground' or at least the seat of wrath and fright," exclaimed Augusta student Robert Whitehead. Because of this outbreak, the faculty voted to adjourn the college and urged students to leave the town as soon as possible. For Whitehead and other students, this situation presented a true dilemma: stay and potentially catch cholera, or leave and have to travel through a region where the disease had already spread. Whitehead revealed this conflict when he reasoned, "Perhaps we had better be here amid friends and acquaintances . . . [than] in a place of strangers, where medical aid would be afforded to patients of long standing sooner than to us. At no time does the wish 'May you die amid your kindred' come more forcibly to our mind than now—never before did we know the great benevolence of that benediction."[27]

Whitehead's fear of dying away from home was justified. The medical technology of the day could not always save students who became ill at college. This stark reality had quite a shaping effect on classmates and friends of the deceased. University of Virginia student Edward Anderson demonstrated some of the possible depth of emotion during an epidemic in 1857. Six students died, including Tom Nelson, whom Anderson considered his best friend. In describing Nelson's fate, Anderson wrote, "When he first felt the fever coming on he went home & was sick then & they say that when he was told he could not survive he was perfectly resigned[,] gave all the orders about his funeral[,] & died like a true christian." Perhaps in reflecting on the life that could have been for his friend, Anderson realized his own mortality: "Poor fellow life was opening to him under its brightest auspices, he was engaged to be married to a daughter of Dr. Chas. Minor of Charlottesville & had every prospect of succeeding well in his profession."[28]

Physical illness clearly had a place in the antebellum college environment, but some students also had bouts with mental illness. Probably the most common problem was clinical depression, called "melancholy" or "depression of spirits" in the day. Students had to endure major life changes during their time in college, and often that fact was enough to bring mental stress to the youngster. University of Virginia student Leroy Broun wrote about a friend and fellow student named Jim, whom he claimed was suffering from a "remarkable depression of spirits." He explained that doctors had diagnosed "fear" as the prominent trait of his "disease." Jim's depression seemed to manifest itself in a fear about his spiritual salvation. Broun explained that Jim would have "the preacher (Scott) to see him three or four times" and that Jim would seem "very penitent." Then, after his depression receded for a few days, Jim would lay "aside all religious feelings." This erratic behavior also appeared in other areas. Jim, for instance, wrote home to his father to come get him, then composed a new letter the next day saying he had changed his mind. Ultimately, the worried parent took his son home to recuperate.[29]

Of course, not all illnesses resulted in death, nor had such grave consequences as depression. More common was for students to trade colds and coughs, or even the quinsy, which resulted in a severe sore throat. In fact, one problem faced by many college students was tooth decay and disease. Edward Anderson told the story of his dental adventure in letters home to his parents. In 1858 he wrote that he had gone to the dentist to have his teeth "attended to" and that the dentist had explained that one of the teeth "would have to be drawn." Anderson decided to delay the pulling because it happened to be New Year's Day and he "expected a good dinner." He explained, however, that he could not put off the operation for long because the dentist had exposed the nerve while attempting to clean the tooth. "Indeed," asserted Anderson, "once he struck it with so much violence that I nearly jumped out of the chair." In the meantime the cavity remained filled with cotton inserted by the dentist to prevent the "air getting in." Anderson prolonged his agony for at least a week—six days later he wrote another letter home, in which he confessed, "I have not yet had my tooth pulled out: I cling to it as an old friend who has done me many a good service & gone through much pleasure with me but I am afraid the time has most come for us to part company now." Presumably he did just that. No further mention of his tooth occurs in subsequent letters.[30]

Anderson's reticence to have his tooth pulled was common. In an era before anesthetics, people went to the dentist only as a last resort. But for some students pain was not the reason for their avoidance of dental treatment. University of Virginia student G. K. Miller provided an example when he wrote about his roommate in 1860. He explained that the young man had been sick for the last week with a severe toothache. What made his predicament particularly bad was that his pain was in his front teeth. Therefore, the student's greatest fear was not the pain of having the teeth removed, but the possibility that if he did so, no woman could be attracted to him, ruining all future chances of marriage.[31]

Another area of the college environment—and one closely related to dental issues—was dining. Students had to design creative solutions for problems related to dining; and in this way they helped to design their own environment. These adolescents had enjoyed the meals cooked for them at their homes for their entire lives. Now they had to adjust to a more corporate dining atmosphere, whether in a private boarding facility or at the college dining room. This fact does not mean that they did not eat well. In fact, in the early 1820s when Jefferson Davis was a student at Transylvania University in Kentucky, his typical fare was a heavy breakfast, consisting of coffee, milk, bread, and butter; and either steak, mutton, bacon, or salt-meat. His midday dinner included bread, meat, soup, and vegetables. His evening meal was more modest, consisting of tea, milk, and corn mush.[32]

Despite the abundance of food in most cases, the fare still would never measure up to home cooking. The food gave students several reasons to complain. For instance, in 1860 Andrew McCollam of Centenary College in Louisiana griped to his father that he had to board with thirty-nine other students at the president's home. "You may imagine the chatter there is at meal time," he wrote; then he added, "the fare is abominable but as good as any to be found in Jackson or vicinity."[33]

For some who dined on the campus, complaints could be even stronger. In 1838, Virginia's Hampden-Sidney College adopted a policy that all students had to board together at the college's Steward's Hall. One student, Robert Dabney, expressed great concern that the food would be "miserably bad," because the college would not have to compete for students as had been the case between the boardinghouses. He further worried that if so many young men had to eat together, disorder and poor manners would be the result. He wrote that in previous such experiments where students had to dine together, the result was "much disorder, and snatching, that without any exaggeration, it was impossible to get enough wholesome, eatable, food, unless you would condescend to snatch & scuffle like a pig." The students at the college, he reported, were universally against the plan.[34]

Even in situations in which students liked the food, they found something to complain about. University of North Carolina student William McLaurin wrote in 1859 that he had "excellent fare" at his boardinghouse, adding a pessimistic note questioning whether the good food "will hold out so all the time." Even McLaurin's general compliment cloaked a gripe: "I never saw a place that there are as many chickens used as there are at this place[.] They have them at every meal[,] fried[,] stewed[,] or baked. I think they must spring up in the woods spontaneously."[35]

Within this world of food, college students demonstrated their move away from childhood toward adulthood. In many cases they showed their independence by finding creative solutions to their eating difficulties. For instance, University of North Carolina student William Mullins had a problem with the *timing* of his meals. He explained: "We eat supper at a quarter past five, breakfast at eight, and dinner at one. This arrangement is very inconvenient and produces unpleasant and injurious results. Supper succeeds dinner at so short an interval, that we have no appetite, and eat but very little, whereas it is important that we should eat plentifully at this meal, as *fifteen* hours pass before we eat again." Nevertheless, Mullins was able to get around this problem by eating a second supper every night at a local boarding establishment he called "old Nancy's." He concluded: "turkeylegs and warm coffee are always pleasant at night, when one is hungry, and I can always find them at Miss Nancy's."[36]

In another situation, students at Emory and Henry College had grown tired of the repetitious fare of their college meals. For several days in a row their meals had consisted solely of mutton and soup. Some of the students got together and put up a flyer that read "Sheep-meat, Sheep-meat for dinner. And fly-soup." They also drew a picture of one of the professors "drawing a sheep up to the slaughter block." Finally, they signed the poster "Starvation." The faculty and administration chastised the students for this display, but the flyer received its desired result. "It seems the insulting notice of yesterday had a good effect. Apple pie for dinner," wrote one of the student participants.[37]

In between the regular meals, antebellum college students also enjoyed special treats. Ice cream was a favorite, if it could be obtained. At the University of North Carolina, several students even had a gambling ring, in which the losers had to treat the winners to ice cream and lemonade. After losing one such bet, a student took his friends to a local establishment and was disappointed to find that it had no ice cream. All was not lost, because they were able to settle for sherbet. Of course another major source of "extra" treats was through packages from home. Students often relied heavily on baked goods and other treats sent by their families. In 1857, University of Virginia student Edward Anderson wrote that several boxes from his Georgia home had recently arrived safely. He reported that he and his friends "set to work to open them & examine the contents—with which we were very much pleased as they assured us against starvation for some time to come."[38]

Students also used the slave environment of the South to obtain extra food. In southern slavery there always existed an underground economy in which slaves earned extra money outside of the master's knowledge. Everyone knew about this arrangement, and college students took advantage of it. When William B. Whitfield and several of his classmates were fishing one Saturday, they got hungry and sought out an old slave, whom they saw heading home for dinner. They told the man to get them something to eat. The man said that his master would not allow him to bring them food, but that he "would do the best that he could." After about an hour, the slave appeared with a large bundle under his arm. The boys gave the man a quarter, and he laid before them "some meat and bread together with a bottle of butter-milk." As he left, the slave urged the young men to hide the bottle where his master would not find it.[39]

The institution of slavery in the American college environment was, of course, unique to the Old South. Although not all students came from slaveholding families, they generally accepted slavery as a part of the college atmosphere. As with other institutions in the Old South, colleges and universities functioned with the help of slaves. For most students, however, slaves were a rather invisible but useful part of their college experience. When William Whitfield and his friends had gone fishing, they had not planned on asking a slave for food, but they nevertheless relied on a slave to get some for them when they realized they were hungry.

Most southern college students came from an aristocratic background, and slavery had been a major part of their childhood development. A common theme in letters home was for the students to ask about the "servants." Georgian Edward Anderson closed each of his letters with different versions of this request, including "Remember me to all the servants & to Laddy, Pompey, &c."; "Remembrances to servants"; and "remember me to the servants all."[40] Similarly, University of Virginia student J. F. Henry went even further, signing his letters, "Give my love to all the folks both white & black."[41]

Some students even brought their slaves with them to college. In the 1820s, Transylvania University student and later abolitionist Cassius Clay kept a servant. This arrangement proved successful until the servant fell asleep one night on the stairs where he had been shining Clay's boots. The slave had "stuck a tallow candle to the steps . . . and the flames went like powder."[42] A more lucrative arrangement came to Hampden-Sidney College student William G. Field, who owned a thirteen-year-old slave named Martin. At first, Field hired out Martin to a plantation and used the proceeds for spending money. When Martin turned fifteen, Field sent for him and hired him out to the seminary steward for the next year at a rate of seventy dollars.[43]

At other institutions the use of slave servants came as part of the tuition and board fees. For students living at the University of Virginia, a black slave entered their rooms at 6 A.M. with a pitcher of water. The servant started a fire in the grate and then polished the student's shoes. After the student dressed and left for breakfast, the slave made the bed, swept the room, and then carried out the ashes from the fireplace.[44]

Clearly, these students lived in a privileged environment in which slavery thrived. In fact, they often found amusement in the fact that many of the southern college faculty were not from the South and did not understand the slave system. In 1850, Emory and Henry College student James Gwyn wrote: "I witnessed a funny quarrel between Prof. Longley and one of the negroes."

> *Longley:* "Why didn't you catch those chickens I ordered last night?"
> *Washington:* "I had some blacking to do at the college."
> *Longley:* "Will you promise me now to obey in the future?"
> *Washington:* "Well I don't know."
> *Longley* (seizing a board): "Will you promise me Washington to mind in the future?"
> *Washington:* "I'll tell you some other time."
> *Longley:* "Tell me now (beating him). Will you?"
> *Washington:* "Some other time."
> *Longley:* "When will that time be?"
> *Washington:* "When two black Sundays come together."

The professor dropped the board and left exasperated. Gwyn's analysis of the exchange was, "Negroes are very saucy in this country. Especially so here, in the hands of Yankees."[45]

The type of brutality reported in the accounting of this story was common in the slave system and, therefore, on southern college campuses. This type of oppression and violence was also a learned behavior for the college students. For an adolescent to witness even a "Yankee" professor use force and violence when dealing with a slave would have a lasting effect on that young mind.

Two incidents reported by Basil Manly II, president of the University of Alabama, further illustrate this type of treatment of slaves. In 1844 three students walked home after a night of drinking. They came across the president's servant, Augustus, and beat him with a stick. In his account of the incident, the president made sure to add that the attack was "without provocation." One of the students had to answer for this action before the faculty, but acted "unapologetic," prompting the faculty to suspend him. They readmitted him, however, when the boy agreed to pay the one-dollar doctor's bill and to pay monetary reparations to Augustus in the amount of three dollars.[46]

Despite Manly's disgust at the violence his students had used, the inference is that had the attack been "provoked" then it would have been acceptable. What constituted provocation could be anything from outright defiance on the part of a slave to "sauciness" as stated by James Gwyn. In 1846, Manly recorded another incidence of violence against a slave, but this time Manly committed the act. He explained: "This afternoon, the college boy, Sam, behaved very insolently to Thos. B. Green; and refused to measure . . . a load of coal which Green had brought. By order of the Faculty he was chastized, in my room, in their presence. Not seeming humbled, I whipped him a second time, very severely."[47]

Violence against slaves, therefore, played a role in the college environment, and was part of the education received by southern college students. These adolescent, privileged young men of the South were learning the rules of their adult society. One of the most important lessons regarding slavery, however, was one that pervaded the society. Namely, in a culture guided by a code of honor, slaves could have no honor. Young white men of the South learned this argument from the time they were born. For those who lived on plantations, daily dealings with slaves reinforced the belief that slaves had no honor (if they had honor, then how could they be slaves?). When these young men went to college, the idea became more, not less, pronounced. They lived and worked with scores of other privileged (honorable) white men.[48]

An incident from the University of Mississippi perhaps best illustrates this concept of honor as it related to slavery at the university. On May 11, 1859, when Chancellor Frederick A. P. Barnard was away, two students entered his home with the intention of raping one of his female servants. One of the students, identified only as "H," beat a young slave woman named Jane so badly that she had visible bruises for two months. One of the professors witnessed the two young men as they left the house. Barnard soon learned their names and ordered that "H" be arraigned before the faculty at a meeting. The faculty passed the following resolution: "That, although the Faculty are morally convinced of Mr. H's guilt, yet they do not consider the evidence adduced to substantiate the charge as sufficient legally to convict him." Nevertheless, Barnard convinced the student to withdraw, and then denied him readmittance the next semester.

For the next year the university would be embroiled in this controversy. The issue, however, was not the brutalization of the slave woman, but whether Barnard had allowed the testimony of a black woman to be used against a young gentleman of the South. Again, the southern code of honor insisted that no African American possessed honor; therefore, Jane's word was worthless. Barnard insisted that he had made his decision based on the professor's testimony, not Jane's. It finally took a hearing of the board of trustees to acquit Barnard.[49]

Because these students followed the same honor ethic that guided southern society as a whole, a student's appearance was paramount. Therefore, financial expenses also played a leading role in determining the college environment. Whether from an aristocratic background or not, these adolescents' financial needs were quite extensive—usually more extensive than their parents had anticipated.

In 1833, Randolph-Macon College student Robert Cutler chided his father's knowledge of college expenses. "I was somewhat surprised to see your ignorance of the money necessary at college," he wrote. "The making of a coat here costs six dollars and a half and for my life I have but six dollars." Young Cutler had evidently started out with much more than six dollars, but had spent it on other necessities. He justified his spending habits, stating, "I have spent less money than any student in College to my own certain knowledge."[50]

Cutler's concern about having enough money for a coat illustrates the importance of clothing within this "honorable" world of appearances. Students suffered tremendous pressure to dress properly in front of their peers. Often this dress was quite elaborate. Jefferson Davis, president of the Confederacy, reflected on dress at Transylvania University, where he was a student in the early 1820s. "I was fastidious in the manner of dress," he remembered. Full dress, he explained, consisted of "canton crepe trousers, buff-colored buckskin boots, dark blue or black swallow tail coat with brass buttons which were sometimes flat and sometimes bullet-shaped, white waist-coat, shirt ruffled at the bosom and sleeves, very stiff and high-standing collars, and the white or black broad silk cloth." Ever aware of the fact that his clothes identified him as a gentleman of means, Davis even went to the extreme measure of demanding extra starch in his collars. He concluded: "I used to beg my laundress, Tiny, to starch my collars so stiff that they would draw blood from my ears."[51]

There is no doubt that clothing was a substantial expense for some of the more wealthy students. William G. Field of Hampden-Sidney College kept a list of his expenses during a year at college. His total expenses, including tuition, room, and board came to $602.88. Nearly half of that total, however, came from clothing purchases during the year, which included: "1 suit of green cashmere, coat, pants, and silk vest" ($31); "1 pair of fancy pants" ($6); "1 white vest" ($2.50); "1 suit of grey cashmere coat pants and vest" ($22); "1 pair of cashmere pants" ($5); "1 fine black suit coat, pants, and silk vest" ($40); "1 suit of spring goods coat, pants, and silk vest" ($23); "coat and pants, fancy drilling" ($8); "1 white linen coat" ($3.50); "1 white vest" ($4); "renovating clothes" ($9.50); "3 pair of calf skin boots" ($21); "2 pair of calf skin shoes" ($5); "4 pair of pumps" ($10); "1 pair of patent leather gaiters" ($5); "1 Panama" hat ($2.75); "1 black slouch" hat ($2.75); "1 white fir" hat ($3); "1 straw" hat ($1.25); "1 pair of gauntlets [gloves]" ($2); "1 pair of dog skin" gloves ($1.25); "1 pair of black kid" gloves ($1.25); "1 pair of silk" gloves ($2.25); "1 pair of French buckskin" gloves ($1); "20 linnen collars" ($5); "12 pair of white cotton socks" ($4); "8 pair of colored cotton socks" ($3); "6 pair of drawers" ($8); "6 white linnen handkerchiefs" ($3); "4 fancy silk hand-kerchiefs" ($4); "2 silk cravats (Black)" ($3.50); and "1 silk scarf (Black)" ($3.50).[52]

Field's expenditures for clothing represent the extreme. Not all students had the means, or at least the financial support from home, to make such extravagant purchases for their wardrobes. Robert Dabney had attended Hampden-Sidney College in the decade before Field, but then transferred to the University of Virginia. Dabney's father was deceased, and although his mother owned a small plantation, she never had large profits. As a result, Dabney only infrequently had spending money at college and he wore "homespun" clothes rather than tailor-made suits like Field. In an 1840 letter to his mother, Dabney complained that one of his old Hampden-Sidney friends, a young man of considerable wealth, had also transferred to the university, but would no longer associate with him. "I believe he has relapsed into the deathlike aristocratic coldness which characterizes his family (the Carrington's) and . . . he would be much belittled by an intimacy with anyone who wears homespun breeches."[53] Even with this condemnation of the aristocratic students, Dabney had conformed to peer pressure at an earlier stage in his college career. Only a few years before, while he was still at Hampden-Sidney College, he wrote to his brother that he would not wear a particular coat because it was not the style worn by the other boys. He explained: "I could not wear a coat of such outlandish form with out subjecting myself to ridicule & other inconveniences."[54]

The administration at some colleges tried to negate this sort of peer pressure by requiring uniforms. Student reaction to this type of requirement was mixed. When Hampden-Sidney considered the action, Robert Dabney was pleased. On the other hand, students at other institutions saw the obligation as proof that the faculty was not of the aristocratic class. In describing the president of Augusta College in Kentucky, student Robert Whitehead wrote that he was "a very plain man in dress and manners." Whitehead explained that as a result the president had been "trying for several years to have a cheap uniform in College and came very near to obtaining his object at the last meeting of the trustees." Whitehead reported that the trustees passed regulations "enacting that, No student shall wear broad cloths and prohibiting them also from wearing ruffle shirts; they are permitted to wear jeans, casinetts or satinetts for there are some right extravagant students which Doct Ruter [the president] considers as a disrepute to the College."[55]

Whether used to buy clothes to fit in, or to purchase extra goods for their enjoyment, money was a constant topic discussed in letters from students to their parents. Students found several creative ways to ask for more money. These requests, however, always centered around the attempt to demonstrate responsible spending. Even though most of these students were adolescents, they wanted to appear to be responsible adults. In 1836, Robert Dabney expressed a common dilemma that faced college students—high prices. He wrote to his mother: "Every thing seems to be selling at double of what it is worth here, and every body seems to conspire to extract money from our pockets." Unlike most students, Dabney also stated that he was not asking for more money, assuring her, "I do not intend this as a preface to a request for more money.

I know your circumstances, and I know that you have given me as liberal an allowance as you can afford."[56]

Other college students, however, used as many techniques as possible to convince their parents to send more money. John Jones, at the University of North Carolina, tried to enlist the help of his older brother. Jones built his case as follows: "When I left home Papa gave me forty five dollars," he began. "I paid thirty for board, eleven for room rent and tuition[,] three for bed hire[,] and one I sent to salem last Saturday for candles which has left me completely unmonied." He explained that as a result he owed money for "necessities," such as $4.00 for "the washing of my clothes," $3.50 for "the expense of our last Ball," and $2.50 for "servant hire." He ended his letter stating that he wanted his father to send him some extra money. He asked his brother to make the request for him because the brother had gone to the University of North Carolina and would understand a student's financial needs.[57]

Edward Anderson used a more subtle method to ask for money from his parents. He played on their fear and parental worries about him being so far from home. Anderson attended the University of Virginia, but his home was in Georgia. His parents had expressed concern over reports they had heard of an epidemic (perhaps yellow fever) that was spreading at the University of Virginia. They had advised their son to leave Charlottesville and travel to Fredericksburg to stay with relatives until the epidemic had ceased. Anderson's response to his parents contained a not-so-hidden appeal for funds. He first assured them that reports of an epidemic had been inflated. He further offered, however, "I would have liked to follow your counsel in your last letter & go to Fredericksburg but in the first place I did not think the fever bad enough to call for such a step & in the next from the depths of my pantaloon pockets I heard the mournful cry of 'no change' but I can assuage you that *if* your counsel had been in the form of an order and *if* my pockets had not returned so distressing a cry I would have gone most willingly not from fear of the fever but because of I am heartily sick of this place & everything connected with it." (It is important to note that young Anderson wrote this in the middle of taking final examinations in all of his courses.)[58]

Of the many challenges antebellum southern college students faced on their journey toward respect and acceptance in the adult world, the college environment was one of the toughest. They had to navigate the many facets of this environment and find creative solutions to the complex nature of leaving home and building a life separate from family. On this journey through the college environment, they faced the challenges of travel, the inevitability of homesickness, the variety of accommodations, the threat of illnesses, the unfamiliarity of corporate dining, the dilemma of slavery, and the constant need of financial support. Nevertheless, by facing each of these challenges, within the rules of honor and propriety demanded by the southern society, these students used the college environment to shape themselves as adults.

In the midst of all these conflicts, students also could occasionally sit back and reflect on the special nature of their existence in a college setting. University of North Carolina student William Sydney Mullins illustrates this point best. As he sat alone, writing in his diary after an evening of food, cigars, and conversation, he listened to the sound of some fellow students playing the flute. He recorded the scene: "The night is beautiful: the chapel and bellfrey stand out plainly in the bright moonlight and the grove has a splendid appearance. . . . The college buildings look better by moonlight than the garish blaze of day and combined with the music, the scene becomes exquisite. The clock has just struck eleven. How solemn it sounds at night." As turbulent as the college environment could seem, Mullins and many of his fellow southern collegians did ultimately find solemnity in their college experiences.

CHAPTER 3

Sowing Oats and Growing Up

AMUSEMENTS, ENTERTAINMENT, AND RELATIONSHIPS

EVEN THOUGH antebellum southern college students spent a considerable amount of time dealing with their studies, college life offered so much more outside of the classroom. These young men, away from home for the first time, found creative ways to occupy their attentions, to explore their newfound freedom, and to build relationships that would last a lifetime. It is in this extracurricular world, however, that the dichotomy of adolescence can best be seen. In each of these activities, college student behavior varied wildly from childish actions to mature, adult reasoning.

One of the most practiced activities in the extracurricular lives of the students was correspondence. Maintaining a connection to home and the familiar was an important aspect of life in college. For young men who were busy breaking the tie to home and childhood, hearing news from home was still of primary importance. As one student put it, "It helps a boy here, when his spirits are getting a little down by such a monotonous course as college life seems to be, you cant tell how much, to receive a kind letter from home, stating that all are well, &c."[1]

Students wrote letters to inform parents and loved ones about their academic progress, about their physical and mental well-being, to express their newly gained knowledge, and to talk about friendships they had made while away from home. Sometimes the letters reflected the real life at college, and other times they reflected a more idealized, "parent-friendly" version. In the former category, Hector James McNeill wrote to his parents the following: "I am so much upset by noise &c &c thay [that] I cannot settle my mind long enough to wright you a se[n-]sible letter or at least a satisfactory one."[2] Most students, however, would not admit that the rowdiness of college was so great that writing letters was difficult.

Other letters reflected the maturation process that the students were undergoing. The young writers would share new political ideas, or discuss academic subjects they were learning. Some students used letters home to "instruct" younger siblings about the ways of the world. University of North Carolina student David Lees wrote just such a letter to his younger brother, Hugh, in 1824. The collegian was concerned about his younger sibling's letter-writing style and ability. "Permit me here to make a remark of some importance," he began in earnest. "It is necessary that a letter at least in its outward appearance should be neat, that it consist of common letter paper, be backed correctly, & be folded up in the usual manner & of the usual size, as that a young person should be neatly and fashonably dressed when he appears in the company of strangers."

As Lees continued this letter, he broadened the target audience to all of his family members. He penned: "This Hugh I intend to apply to all of you, as I often get letters from you which are on coarse, unsuitable paper, & which have the directions on the back put on the wrong place, & the places to which they are directed incorrectly spelt." His main complaint about how his family "spelt" centered around the way they addressed letters to him. He complained that his family would "spell Chapel Hill thus Chapilhill, others thus Chapple Hill, & some times thus Chaplehill. Now none of these is correct. This is the way to write it, *Chapel Hill,* making two words instead of one, each of which begins with a capital letter & the first having but one *p* in it." His final advice was about how to fold letters properly. Generously, he offered, "I believe I generally fold and back my letters in the fashonable way; if you can there fore condescend to take mine as patterns[,] for it is of *importance* to write a *nice* letter & any person can succeed who takes the necessary pains."[3]

As important as letter writing was to college students, letter *reading* was all the more cherished. Letters represented one of the few remaining ties to home and to childhood. If students went for a long period without correspondence from family and friends, they often became depressed and expressed their dissatisfaction with the situation. In 1855,

Henry Bryan wrote of his concerns this way: "My Dear Ma, I have been expecting a letter from home for sometime, and as it seems that you have all quit the business of letter writing, I thought I would write and see if I could not persuade you to resume it, as it is very agreable, to say the least of it, to hear occasionaly from you."[4]

Despite the importance of the connection to home through letters, college students also enjoyed their new freedom. Their activities often reflected an almost carefree approach to life away from home and in the company of other young men their same age. This is not to say that these young men had no sense of adult responsibilities and expectations. Indeed, they often created social rules and obligations within their peer groups to demonstrate their coming of age in the adult world. At the same time, their amusements often reflected their continued youthfulness.

A great example of the dichotomy of adolescence can be seen in seasonal frivolity among college students. The summer months stirred the students' youthful spirits. The season brought a frenzy of activity from these young men who had been cooped up for long winter months with their books. Independence Day often proved to be a choice time for whimsical behavior. Robert Dabney, while at Hampden-Sidney College, wrote that he and his fellow students celebrated Independence Day "by throwing up balls of cotton steeped in spirits of turpentine, and set on fire." With these homemade fireworks, Dabney and about forty of his friends went to the local girls' boarding school "and threw about these balls, and fired off bombs made by wrapping up large quantities of powder in a great deal of cloth, which made almost as much noise as a cannon."[5]

At another Fourth of July celebration, five University of Alabama students learned a hard lesson about behaving childishly. During a picnic on the Warrior River, these students stripped naked and went for a swim within the sight of the "Gents and Ladies." In the proper adult society of the antebellum South, this type of behavior was unacceptable—even dishonorable. The students involved ended up being reprimanded, but they received leniency because it was judged that the incident was probably no more than "indiscretion" and that the boys had already been punished enough "in the bad notoriety they had acquired."[6]

Just as in summer, college students also found winter activities in which to express their youthful exuberance. When a long cold spell struck Kentucky in 1831, Augusta College student Robert Whitehead reported, "There has been fine scating all the winter and some of the boys have scated a great deal." Whitehead, who had never skated before, did not brave the ice until a few days before he wrote the letter, but he evidently liked it, promising, "I will be ready for next winter."[7]

Some winter activities required a more complex involvement among these young gentlemen of the South. Having grown up under a strict code of honor, southern gentlemen often had to avoid situations that could lead to humiliation or shame. Nevertheless, put several hundred adolescent boys together in the midst of a big snowstorm, and the rules of society get ignored in favor of the potential fun of a snowball fight. Just such a situation occurred at the University of North Carolina in 1841. The usually proper and mature student William Sydney Mullins described it as follows: "A snow in College produces a general suspension of dignity: all classes, Societies, and intimacies are suspended and every man becomes so familiar with his neighbor as to meet him in the array of snow-strife. . . . On our return from supper there was a general melee of snow-fighting, the whole campus being filled with the armies. . . . Suffice it to say, that general merriment prevailed, and all was harmony though several foes of reciprocol hostility were on the *un*tented field."[8] Suspending dignity was worth it for good snowball fun.

In addition to special amusements brought by weather or holidays, students also found significant pleasure in other, more regular activities. Southern boys grew up learning to fish and hunt, and many continued these activities while in college. William Whitfield recorded numerous spontaneous fishing trips in his diary. In 1860 he even reported skipping his literary society meeting to go fishing with two of his friends. The reward for this trip was "about fifty fish" and "an eel."[9] Similarly, Andrew McCollam of Louisiana's Centenary College confessed that bringing his gun to school had been a "great source of pleasure" because he "spent one half of each Saturday in hunting" as a "source of relaxation to me after the studies of the week . . . and for the exercise it gives me and which I would not otherwise take."[10] Hampden-Sidney student William Field also reported that he and his roommate spent almost every Saturday hunting with a local farmer. "We usually hunted all day," he asserted, "carrying a horse with us to bear our provisions and game. We hunted partridges of which there were a great number, but I never succeeded in killing more than fourteen in one day."[11]

Students also filled their spare time in seeking entertainment. Dancing schools and taverns were popular, although often officially off limits to students. At Austin College, in Huntsville, Texas, students frequented a bowling establishment known as "Tin Pin Alley" and W. B. Clark's "Dance Academy," even though the faculty had decreed these places off-limits because of their proximity to a local saloon. On the subject of dancing, Austin College students often found themselves at odds with the faculty, who generally deemed the activity to be sinful and unbecoming. In 1858, two students at the college, Champ and William Hill, organized a dance in the college building in celebration of that year's commencement. These brothers were among the graduating class, and when they announced the dance, excitement erupted from both the students and the faculty. Students clamored to attend; faculty ordered the event to be cancelled. The Hill brothers refused, asserting that they had "the sympathy of the students and the community." When the faculty insisted, all of the graduating seniors withdrew their participation in the commencement exercises. With this escalation of events, the faculty responded by denying diplomas to the Hill brothers. A month later the issue went before the board of trustees, who sided with the students, stating: "Had a more conciliatory course been pursued, we are convinced that the end of discipline might have been accomplished." Taking this decision as a slap in the face, the acting president of the college resigned, disrupting class offerings for months—but the Hill brothers had prevailed.[12]

Horse racing, plays, and traveling entertainers also brought great pleasure to young men at southern colleges. University of Virginia student John Henry reported that Charlottesville had a double attraction in November of 1856. The local theater had a production of Shakespeare's *Richard III*, which Henry criticized as "rather poor," yet he had "a good deal of fun." More exciting to him and his friends, however, was the fact that a traveling "museum" had come to town. For the boys, the highlight of the display was a "bearded woman and some dwarfs."[13]

If the college or university was near the county seat, students often found court day to be of great excitement. Robert Dabney of Hampden-Sidney elaborates: "This is court day in this county and the students have a sort of holiday. They have almost all gone down to the courthouse to hear an electioneering speech from the congressman of this district, and I intend to go as soon as I have gotten through with my letter. There are several students waiting for me now."[14]

Of course, students did not need to have a special occasion or a formal form of entertainment to have a good time. Often they sought to entertain themselves with another pastime of the Old South—alcohol. Pursuit of the pleasures of the bottle on southern college campuses was prolific. These students, who usually arrived at college mere boys, saw consuming spiritous liquors as a way of enjoying their new freedom and expressing their adulthood.

James Dusenbery, of the University of North Carolina, described in his diary several alcohol-related incidents among his friends. "Yesterday was Slade's birth day, he went to Hillsboro & returned in the evening, pretty tight, bringing with him 3 bottles of elegant Nash brandy. Pink & Slade got most *gloriously tight* that night. Myself, with a few others were moderately so." Dusenbery further reported, "Matters went on thus until midnight until Slade began to vomit & we put him to bed. McBee was still high in the wind & began to halloo at some other drunken fellows in the Campus." In another incident, Dusenbery asserted that at a Washington's birthday celebration "The amount of liquor drunk by the students was tremendous. more than 2/3ds of the college were intoxicated." Dusenbery also participated in this revelry, admitting, "Pink & I went over to the East [Building] & were gloriously tight before breakfast. We kept the *thing hot* throughout the day."[15]

The extensiveness of alcohol use evident from these examples was a problem college administrators tried to fight—usually unsuccessfully. To curb student drinking in Chapel Hill, local officials passed a law forbidding the sale of alcohol within two miles of the campus. James Johnston Pettigrew wrote his father in 1844 about how ineffectual this law was: "It is somewhat amusing to see how persons evade the law about selling liquor to the students within two miles of the hill or to any other persons. Some time ago, a man here named Thompson gave a dinner and charged a half dollar for the eating and gave away the liquor. And within the last week a groggery has been established just a little over two miles from the hill."[16] Students were also ingenious in finding ways to get alcohol. William Blackledge Whitfield even determined to make his own. His father had told him about "a certain 'California increase' out of which beer can be made by pouring sweetened water on it and it increases every time it is used." Whitfield obtained some of this "California increase," presumably some sort of yeast, from his landlady, and then he bought molasses to make beer. His goal was for his friends and himself to "enjoy ourselves finely drinking beer."[17]

Not all students indulged in this particular vice. In fact, by mid-century, as the temperance movement grew in the nation, some college students followed suit, pledging not to drink alcohol. In 1861, Roanoke College student Thomas Martin joined the Sons of Temperance organization, which had been holding public meetings in the area. Martin had two reasons for becoming a member of the group. He reasoned, "I thought I could influence some of the students to quit drinking," and he also wished to become free "from the temptation to engage in it myself."[18] Neither Martin, nor Roanoke College, were unique. Numerous institutions throughout the South had temperance societies, although memberships did not rival the number of students who did not join. By the mid-1850s, anti-drinking advocates at the University of Virginia constructed Temperance Hall on the university grounds. The university adopted a policy that students who grievously transgressed the laws against drinking could either leave the university or sign a pledge with the Temperance Society. Many students signed the pledge so as to stay at college.[19]

Another favorite pastime of students that helped to create for them a sense of adulthood was the use of tobacco. Students chewed and smoked tobacco in great quantities. Most rooms held a spittoon, and smoking pipes and cigars made many feel quite mature. William Sydney Mullins described one evening of merriment with his friends. The boys had used the excuse of a lunar eclipse in 1841 to go out to have an oyster supper. One of the young men in the group "procured a bottle of peach liquer" and the boys "had some fine fun at his room." As the evening came to an end, Mullins reported, "After a good smoke, and watching the eclipse pass off the moon, I went to bed, about eleven, in very fine spirits, and soon fell into the rich luxury of glorious dreams."[20] Other students expressed similar sentimentality when it came to their tobacco. "I've just taken a good smoke, with a right fair pipe I have," wrote one student to a girl back home. He continued that "while sitting back puffing away in my room, I was strongly reminded of *home,* & last summer, when I used to get my *pipe* you know sometimes & puff a while & you know, hear you a French lesson."[21]

Tobacco usage was so prevalent in southern society that many students engaged in it with the assistance of their relatives back home. In a letter to his mother, University of Virginia student Edward Anderson reminded her to send what he believed to be a necessity in college: pipe stems. He wrote that the stems should be made from cane root. After receiving a package from her that did not include the requested items, he complained, "I was a little disappointed at not finding the pipe stems in the box . . . as you told me you would send them soon & I had promised several away. please dear Mother try & remember to send them to me in the next box you send on & have them gotten at once as if you wait til the sap begins to flow they are not so good." Despite his mother's negligence, young Anderson did not have to go into total nicotine withdrawal, because in the same letter he wrote: "Thank Uncle John kindly for his present of the cigars." Finally, in a letter to his mother a few weeks later, Anderson included a postscript that thanked her for the pipe stems, calling them "beautiful" except that they were somewhat "disfigured."[22]

Cigars played another important role in the activities of antebellum southern college students—that of currency for gambling debts. Cigars, among other items, became common fodder for budding gamblers on the campus. Students would bet on almost anything. Horse racing was a popular pastime, but these young collegians would also place bets on mundane issues of the day. An election year was always a particular target for university gambling. William Sydney Mullins of the University of North Carolina went so far as to place bets on the specific details of the presidential election of 1840. For example, he bet one classmate two dozen cigars that "North Carolina does not give the Harrison Electoral Ticket as large a majority as that which Jno. M. Morehead obtained as

Governor." He bet the same student "4 doz. cigars to 2 doz. cigars that Pennsylvania does not elect the Harrison Electoral Ticket." Mullins won many of the wagers, and he used the proceeds to treat several of his friends to an oyster supper. In describing the supper, he commented that he "shall soon commence my attacks on the numerous cigars, which will be due." He added: "Really it is very fine to enjoy, in addition to our [the Whigs'] great triumph, oysters and cigars. It imparts new interest to the Western Hero's [William Henry Harrison's] election, that it brings, with its advantages to the nation, peculiar pleasure to me."[23] Mullins would later put his political acumen to work in a different manner—he served eight consecutive terms in the South Carolina state legislature.

Student reactions to the freedom they found in college varied. Some, like Mullins, saw college as an opportunity to engage in the trappings of the adult world—to indulge in the vices present for gentlemen in the southern society. Other students, however, recognized problems with the many temptations their newfound independence at college afforded them. In 1851, University of North Carolina student Bartholomew Fuller wrote an essay entitled "The Dangers of College Life." In it he asserted that when a young man left his home for college, "he feels himself at liberty as he thinks to act *for* himself, and the consequence in most cases, is a departure from those principles of moral conduct, which have been instilled in his mind from early youth." Among the dangers Fuller warned about were "extravagance," "idleness," "disrespect toward one's superiors," and "neglect of duties." He also wrote that another danger is "that which is called in common parlance 'spreeing.'"[24]

This danger that Fuller called spreeing could also be labeled "frolics," "romps," or "fun," depending on one's perspective. For many students this type of behavior typified adolescence. They found new ways to cling to their childhood by enjoying immature merriment with other boys. Sometimes these sprees were organized events, while more often they erupted from spontaneous activities among a group of students.

Examples of "organized sprees" would be where an event or activity was planned in advance, or was held on a regular basis. The University of Virginia, for instance, held an annual event in which the students elected the "ugliest man" from among themselves. The lucky fellow had to accept a fifteen-dollar pair of boots and give a humorous speech. Another example from the University of Virginia was "Laughing Gas Day." The chemistry professor would administer laughing gas to a previously selected student, who then would perform antics before the student body while laughing hysterically on the university Lawn. The university discontinued Laughing Gas Day when one student under the influence of the gas engaged in what they termed "improper behavior."[25]

Most student frolic, however, was of the unorganized variety. In January 1848, for instance, some students at the University of Alabama used a rope to pull a large calf onto the roof of the university's Rotunda. By pushing and pulling, they forced the calf to the apex of the building's dome and tied it to a lightning rod.[26] A popular amusement at South Carolina College was called "blackriding." The students wore black robes and masks and would ride horses around the campus carrying torches and make as much noise as possible. Similarly, at several universities students often engaged in what they called the "calathump." The goal of the calathump was for students to use any instrument they could get their hands on (musical or otherwise) and make a tremendous noise in the middle of the night. Real triumph came when the event roused the faculty. University of Virginia student John Henry described one this way: "The students had a 'Calothump' here the other night, about fifty of them masked themselves up, and came up on the Lawn & built a big fire & made more noise than you have ever heard in your life."[27]

Masks played an important role in these childish activities. During the day, students publicly portrayed themselves as upright, mature gentlemen of the South. According to the code of honor to which they adhered, these young gentlemen, therefore, could not be seen behaving in an immature activity.

Related to the issue of honor and identity was another area of student frolic: playing pranks on fellow students. Many pranks centered on the idea of hidden identities. When Robert Dabney was a new student at Hampden-Sidney, a fellow student came to his room "dressed like a negro and having his face blacked, to sell cherries." Dabney reported that several other students who were in on the ruse had "accidentally" dropped in, and they all assured him "that he was a real negro." The young prankster finally ran off with Dabney's Bible, but Dabney felt confident the book would be returned. He concluded, "They are always playing a great many such triks upon new students."[28]

A year later, Dabney reported a further incidence of using blackface as a prank. This time, however, the target was not new students, but the girls attending "Mr. Root's Young Ladies Seminary" down the road from the college. Dabney declared, however, that the two students who had performed the prank "were discovered"—doubtless, much to their shame.[29]

Other targets of student pranks were classmates who set themselves apart—particularly religious students—and, of course, faculty members. In the former category, James Gwyn, a religious student at Emory and Henry College, recorded an incident he decided was a prank against himself by other students. He described a conversation in which a classmate told him he believed in ghosts. Gwyn wrote: "He mentioned many incidents to which he was an eye witness, and as I have all confidence in his veracity, and altogether doubt the existence of ghosts, was not a little perturbed." Gwyn went on to relate that one of the main spectral "events" was the mysterious opening and closing of doors in their lodging rooms. The student even said that he had seen Gwyn's door open by itself when no one else was around. After the conversation ended, Gwyn went back to his room. As he was thinking about the "supernatural" conversation, his room door flew open twice. Gwyn's skepticism, however, never wavered. He wrote: "I must believe that it was either some of the students or that these rooms are so situated that the wind has a peculiarly affect on them."[30]

Professors also felt the brunt of many student pranks. One example comes from the Virginia Military Institute, where Maj. Thomas Jackson led the students in required military drill. A favorite student prank against Jackson was to secretly place a bell on the artillery caisson. When Jackson's artillery students drilled, the bell rang incessantly, causing Jackson great consternation. Another more serious prank was for students to pull the linchpins off of the cannon wheels. When the students turned the cannons during drill, the wheels would fall off. At first Major Jackson thought the linchpins were defective; after several similar incidents he realized it was a prank and arrested every student present. That prank never occurred again.[31]

Amusements, entertainment, frolics, and pranks all helped students create a unique adolescent environment. Through these activities, as well as the intellectual bonds created in the classroom, students formed strong relationships in college. They spent much of their time, in fact, either forging new relationships or maintaining old ones.

One of the most influential relationships students built was with their roommates. As can be expected, some roommate arrangements worked out well, and others did not. But for those that succeeded, the roommate bond was often very strong. An example of this was the friendship between William Gibson Field and Phil Jones of Virginia. The two met at the age of fifteen at a preparatory school at Gordonsville, and they became such good friends that they remained roommates for the next eight years, transferring together to Hampden-Sidney College in 1854, and then to the University of Virginia in 1855. Of his relationship with Jones, Field wrote, "with him my intercourse has been more entirely unreserved than with any one else in the world."[32]

Roommates often grew quite close to one another, learning intimate details about each others' lives, families, hopes, and fears. Conversations between roommates filled a significant portion of the students' lives. When George Miller, a Georgian student at the University of Virginia, described his roommate, he wrote that he was "a young gentleman from Alabama by the name of Crook—a good soul as one will find in many a day, tall, lively, tolerably good looking, of a very sociable disposition, with a rare budget of jokes and many quaint sayings." In describing their relationship as roommates, Miller reported: "We live together as happy as two singing birds, have our own pleasure in social chats after our studies are attended to and our pipes called into use. He is a good admirer of the ladies and loves a Georgia miss to distraction."[33]

Beyond the roommate relationship, southern college students also sought to create an "adult" culture of their own that focused on their own peer group and involved a peer-designed code of honor. One of the relational organizations that best facilitated this desire was the student literary debating society. Every southern college and university campus had these student-created and student-run organizations. Robert Dabney explained the nature of these societies to his mother this way: "There are two of them, the Union & Philanthropick, and the students are almost equally divided between them, both in numbers, and talent. Their object is the improvement of their minds by debate and argument. Each member has to pay a few dollars on entrance and with the money they have bought splendid libraries and fitted up their halls beautifully. The libraries are as completely at the command of the members, as if they belonged to them so that for this money you get the use of all the most usefull and interesting books in the world."[34]

Literary societies played a major role in the lives of college students. The main focus of these societies was for student debate, but in reality they involved much more than this. In the literary society, a student could learn leadership skills and organizational relationships. Each campus had at least a pair of these societies, so students learned the value of loyalty to their group, and competition against their rivals. Finally, it was in the literary society that students best learned to create their own sense of honor within the academic setting of the college or university. This honor, at times, put them at odds with the faculty and administrators of the institution, but it prepared them for their futures as southern gentlemen.

In the literary societies, students learned the all-important skills of debate. Most societies held a major debate each week, with one member assigned to argue the affirmative, and another to argue the negative. When a student received such an assignment, he usually spent hours doing research, writing his arguments, and practicing his oration. The finished product was expected to appear authoritative, polished, and extemporaneous. When each debater had concluded his arguments, the society members would engage in more debate, then would cast a vote for the winner. The winning argument would then be entered into the society's log for future reference, in case the question ever arose again.

Debate topics varied from week to week, from school to school, and from era to era. Sample debate questions from various institutions include: from Transylvania University—"Should not the seduction of a female under promise of marriage be punished with imprisonment or death?" (the affirmative team won on this question); from the University of North Carolina (1841)—"Would it be advantageous to the South for the Union to be divided?" (the negative team won on this question); or from Washington College—"Whether it is more advantageous for a young man to read Ancient or Modern History first?" (Ancient History won).[35]

In addition to debates, literary society membership also included requirements to give speeches. These societies, in fact, often furnished the speakers for commencement ceremonies each year. In a letter to a friend, University of Mississippi student R. P. Willing explained in 1854: "We have two fine societies the Hermean and the Phisigma. . . . their object is to furnish the best orators on commencement day. I have joined the Phisigma. We have some very fine speakers in college belonging to both societies."[36]

These orations helped to train students to be strong public speakers and to overcome fears when facing a crowd. Andrew McCollam of Centenary College in Louisiana described his school's "March Exhibition," which featured two days of speeches from literary society students. McCollam represented the Union Literary Society, the rival to the Franklin Literary Society. He recorded: "Before my time for mounting the rostrum came off, I tormented myself with useless fears but at the time I was perfectly self possessed and went upon the stage with out a tremour and acquitted myself quite well for a Soph." He also reported that the audience in attendance exceeded four hundred. He concluded proudly that the Union Literary Society's performance surpassed that of the Franklin, and that they "bore off the palm of victory from the Franklin."[37]

The oration and debate requirements of these societies meant that they had to build significant libraries for the use of their members. Often the student literary society library was larger and more complete than the college library (if the college had a library at all). In 1849, University of Alabama president Basil Manly reported that the two literary societies there—the Erosophic and the Philomathic—owned a combined total of 2,623 books.[38] The presence of so many books certainly helped students in their preparations. Robert Dabney at Hampden-Sidney wrote with pride to his mother, "I can do anything with the library of the Society, which any owner would wish to do." He did clarify that statement, saying he could not "misuse" the books or "throw them away," but he was most excited that he could "read as many as I wish, and at any time I wish." Dabney boasted that the society library contained "about 1800 or 2000 volumes." Grudgingly, however, he admitted that the rival society on campus had "a few more books than we have."[39]

Rivalry and competition between the different societies on a campus was often intense. One of the areas where this clash can best be seen is in recruitment. Dabney described his first encounter with the society rush in a letter to his mother shortly after he arrived at Hampden-Sidney in 1836. "My room is on the third story and on the north side of the house," he reported. "It was secured for me before I arrived by a student from our county named Pleasants, not so much from any friendship towards me, as from the desire to prepossess me in favour of his society." He further explained to her, "The members of both societies have been electioneering me, (as they call it) ever since I arrived, so that I was obliged to make my decision somewhat hastily to save myself from being tormented to death. I joined the one to which the Sheltons belong [Philanthropic]."[40]

Apparently Dabney had no problems with this heavy-handed method of recruiting society members—just months later he rushed new students using the same tactics. He wrote to his mother in November 1836 that she would be surprised that he had taken in a new student as a roommate without knowing anything of the student's "habits." He declared that he did it because he loved his society, "for when we get a new student in the room with us, we are certain of persuading him to join our society. And we learn a true estimate of a mans character from a very short intercourse with him." He added: "I am rarely mistaken in my opinions, and I find that in the case of my room mate I was exactly right."[41]

Similar recruitment tactics occurred at institutions throughout the South. In the early 1850s, for example, one Randolph-Macon student described the intensity of that school's competing literary societies' "rush." He asserted that upon entering the college a new student could expect "Half a dozen young men [to] surround you and overwhelm you with their generosity. 'You need not put yourself to much trouble,' cries one, 'to find a room. I have no *dash* [roommate] and am willing to take you in until you can get furniture!'" With this offer, he continued, "You are overjoyed at such demonstrations of kindness" and you "accept the tender." Next, "Up you go to his room, and you are scarcely comfortably seated when you are introduced to a number of fine fellows each of whom, if you will notice, wear breastpins similar to the one upon the bosom of your friend." All of this maneuvering, he wrote, continued on for three weeks, until the "electioneering state has reached its climax." Then, on a Friday night, "two members of one of the societies come to you and politely request you to give them your name, to propose as a member of their society." When you turn them down, they "leave your room, and some one in the passage cries: 'Well, boys did you get him?' 'No! But we only lost his *money*. He'll never set a river on fire!'" Then two members of the society you plan to join "enter upon a similar errand, and upon their coming out of another passage, a boy cries: 'Did you get him?' 'Yes; and he's a *bustin'* smart fellow too.'" But, now that the recruitment rush is over, the attention and favors disappear, and "your good friend hints to you the propriety of shifting your quarters." He concluded wryly, "Now, strange though it may appear, your popularity is somewhat diminished."[42]

The competition between rival societies also led them to conduct their meetings in secret. Society members had to take oaths vowing to keep the proceedings and practices of their society shrouded. Robert Dabney explained to his brother that the societies at Hampden-Sidney were "secret concerns and I can only tell you that they are associations of students for purposes of mutual improvement." Having meetings closed to members of the rival society occasionally resulted in curiosity between opposing groups, as reflected in a brief diary entry from a University of North Carolina student. "Went to the Society after breakfast but left before it adjourned," he recorded. "The Phis get out a heap sooner than we do." Then he added, "I wonder what is the reason?" The secrecy, however, could also lead to suspicion and complete separation. Dabney asserted that at Hampden-Sidney the "members of the two societies are almost completely withdrawn from each other."[43]

Even with the suspicion, separation, and curiosity, the literary societies represented a significant influence on the lives of antebellum southern college students. In the society, students practiced functioning as adults. There is no doubt that they were still adolescents, and their behavior often reflected their immaturity. But the literary society imposed a group ethic on each student that mirrored the larger ethos that governed the ruling society of the region.

Because students alone operated these literary societies, the organizations came under the criticism of faculty. At Randolph-Macon College, for instance, the board of trustees had given its approval to the creation of two rival societies on the campus. The college's president, Stephen Olin, also gave his grudging approval to the societies, stating that "Some skill and facility in extemporaneous speaking were acquired, for which the ordinary routine of college life affords less favorable opportunities." But Olin also considered them with a healthy dose of suspicion, writing: "The drawbacks upon these benefits were often party spirit, rivalries, jealousies, and suspicions; a loose and vapid style of speaking and writing, contracted in the absence of proper instruction and judicious criticism; and sometimes an undervaluing of prescribed studies."[44]

The gulf between faculty and students can also be seen from the students' perspective in the literary societies. James Gwyn, of Emory and Henry College, attended his society's meeting on September 6, 1850. He had been appointed to argue the affirmative on the esoteric question, "Is whatever is, right?" Interestingly, his opponent was a guest that evening, the president of the college. Gwyn, who was a fairly religious student, did not like the president's arguments. Gwyn wrote that the president "held the ground that the ways of God to man were right, that the ways of man to God were not right. If *whatever* were limited by the former, he answered in the aff. If by the latter, the neg. Rather a dry debate."[45]

This is an interesting bit of commentary. Perhaps it illustrates the basic power struggle between students and faculty. If one replaces the word "God" with "faculty" and the word "man" with "students," then the above arguments still seem to hold the same contentious opinions of faculty and students regarding power, honor, and their position. This analogy can be further seen in another incident with James Gwyn. A few days after his literary society debate with the president, Gwyn was to deliver a senior speech on a topic of his own choosing. On September 11, 1850, he wrote that he had finished writing his oration. The title: "Triumph of Reason over Authority." Perhaps once again the theme belies his attitude about the student-faculty relationship. The independent thought encouraged by the literary societies helped Gwyn and other students like him to develop a sense of their own maturity in thought and to express that sense of independence publicly.[46]

The influence of the societies on the behavior, thinking, and activities of students was near absolute. Because of this sense of connection to the society, and the strength of the relationship to the other boys who were members, students often felt more loyalty to their literary society than to the college as a whole. University of North Carolina student William McLaurin testified that troublemakers there had to conceal their "many little tricks," making it difficult for them to have fun. Their improper behavior was not thwarted by the faculty, argued McLaurin, but by the literary societies, for troublemakers "are more afraid of the Society than they are of the Faculty although the Faculty come down on them like a thousand of brick."[47] Through this type of influence, literary societies helped to prepare students to function in the adult world.

The time spent with literary society classmates was second only to the time and energy students devoted to the opposite sex. Adolescence, of course, is also the age at which puberty strikes, and young men and women begin the search for a mate. Taking hundreds of pubescent young men away from the watchful eyes of their parents—and placing them together to plot and plan—resulted in tremendous amounts of thoughts about sex. For these young men, the southern code of honor taught them a dual standard when it came to relations with women. They were to seek out potential mates by courting women from their own social status, following rigid rules of honorable behavior. But the code and society also instructed them that they were to engage in sexual conquest.[48] Therefore, one of the major relationships built in antebellum southern colleges was between the students and their sexuality.

For many of the younger college students, their attraction to women was a new experience—one to be enjoyed rather innocently. They felt the attraction, wanted to act on that feeling, but only had enough emotional maturity to do so from afar. When George Dabney arrived at the University of Virginia in 1840, for instance, he spent much of his time looking at women out of his window, because "they come out in this good weather like butterflies." At the University of Alabama, more rambunctious students greeted a group of ladies visiting the campus with shouts and calls from their windows. Students also used mirrors to shine the bright reflection of the sun on the women. These childish actions would eventually have serious consequences. Because the faculty considered these activities to be highly insulting to the ladies, they launched an investigation into the identity of the perpetrators. When every student denied any knowledge of the crime, the faculty, knowing the rooms from which the lights had originated, began to suspend the occupants. Finally, several students admitted their involvement, but others reacted violently at night, removing all gates from the campus and placing them in trees, firing pistols, and yelling. The incident finally resulted in several students leaving the university—some voluntarily, others not.[49]

Other young men did not want to appear as mere youths in the presence of ladies, so they focused their attention on cultivating the countenances of gentlemen. Robert Whitehead of Augusta College went so far as to justify his lack of studying in the name of learning how to talk to women. He argued that it was important for him to spend his time socializing with young ladies. "And who shall say, that in the issue, it may not be profitable to spend my time this way," he debated, "as to confine myself closely, always in my closet, to be as unsociable as the cloistered hermit, and after a while to issue hence, at most, a learned clown, ignorant of mankind—credulous as a child—pedantick as a fool . . . frightened by the mere sight of a female—confused, stammering, and silly-looking when introduced into company."[50]

Not all students held the same outlook as Whitehead. Robert Dabney, while a student at Hampden-Sidney College, asserted that "the company of ladies unfits one for study, & therefore I have not taken advantage of every opportunity for getting into company, although these opportunities are very rare."[51]

Most students fell somewhere between Whitehead and Dabney in their attention to the opposite sex. Courtship played an important role in college life. Often it was a communal affair, with several boys working up the courage to approach young ladies as a group. The serenade was a popular, safe method of showing a young lady attention, as it allowed the young men to remain together. William Whitfield described such an event at the University of North Carolina. He and several of his friends got "4 Jews harps, a fiddle, some combs," and an "old camphene can" to serenade Miss Fannie Durham. He reported that "Chum took the camphene can, Moore the shovel & tongs and a jews harp, Thurmond a fiddle. Hunt & myself a comb apiece and a jews harp." When they arrived outside of the young lady's house just before 11:00 o'clock at night, "Thurmond started with 'Yankee Doodle' on the fiddle and we all joined in with our respective instruments." They played long enough for each of them to try the different instruments. They had success, in that "Miss Fannie came to the door and peeped out."[52]

Similar to the serenade was a practice at the University of Virginia known as performing a "dyke." The purpose of this ritual was to embarrass any fellow collegian who was en route to a rendezvous with a sweetheart. Students gathered any noise-making instrument they could find, then ambushed a young man on the path to his fair one. Accompanying him all the way to the young lady's door, these "friends" would make as much noise as humanly possible. Often the young man who was the target of this cacophony had to give a speech before the assembly would allow him to enter the house.[53]

As students became more experienced in the ways of the heart, the more daring weathered the potential ribbing of classmates to pair up with a young woman. One student at Austin College in Huntsville, Texas, recalled with fondness his "Sunday afternoon strolls along the boardwalk of the town, into lover's lane, or through the quiet shadows of the cemetery" with young ladies of the neighborhood.[54] William Burwell of the University of North Carolina reported that on Valentine's Day several of his classmates were sending off "a good many" Valentines to their "ducks" (sweethearts). Other students felt more comfortable in the role of matchmaker. In May of 1850, University of North Carolina student Leonidas Siler wrote to his cousin, Sallie Jarrett, and pronounced his "cousinly love" for her. In his letter, he reported that when the session ended he would be traveling to his Georgia home accompanied by one of his classmates, a Mr. Treadwell from Mississippi. Siler described his friend to Sallie as "intelligent and clever & withal very good looking." He wrote: "I have something to tell you on him that is worth hearing. We made a swap, and you may know how highly he stands in my opinion, by my giving you to him. I want you to see him &

tell me if you do not like him." He encouraged his cousin to come visit with the most earnest plea: "Oh! Sallie, do please come over to Macon. Be sure and come or I shall be so much disappointed. . . . Do, please come! I'll love you better, if I can."[55]

College courtship often reflected the exciting ups and downs of youthful energy and romantic ideas. Many college men enjoyed "playing the field," and did so with vigor and enthusiasm. This setting, however, also made some young men quite fickle with their affections, and their moods and desires changed by the week. This phenomenon is reflected in a series of letters written by University of North Carolina student Arthur McKimmon to a friend from late October through mid-November 1859.

In October, McKimmon had just returned to the university after spending a week at the state fair, where he had enjoyed entertaining a Miss Connelly. He wrote to his friend that "if there ever was a sad mortal I am one. Ever since last Saturday [when he returned to the university] I have had the blues . . . & I feel more like committing suicide than doing anything else." He continued, "Imagine yourself in my situation. Here I am, after spending a week so very pleasantly with the fair sex, in the dullest place in the world surrounded by no associates but those of the masculine gender."

Also in that letter, he reported that many at the university were under the impression that he was "desperately in love with Nick Williams' cousin which to those who were ignorant of the fact I positively denied." He also asserted that he was not "the only one in this condition. . . . The fact is that everyone who attended the fair is looking very melancholy." On November 15, however, McKimmon wrote that things had improved, because he had gone to a party in Hillsboro, North Carolina, and found that Miss Connelly was in town. He was able to escort her to the party and he reported that they had a "nice time." But the next night he had tea with Miss Mary Lillie, Nick Williams's cousin, and talked to her for hours, which, he reported, "did not seem fifteen minutes to me so you conjecture how I enjoyed it."

The next night, he escorted Miss Mary Lillie to a party. By his November 20 letter, it was clear that Arthur was absolutely smitten with "Miss Mary," because he wrote that he had learned she would be shopping in Raleigh when he was to be there. He had begun to worry about competitors for her attentions, including Nick Williams and an unknown law student. He confided, "I am exceedingly anxious to find out who that law student is, for he is the only one of the two that I fear, for if I cannot cut Nick out, I will retire from the field of battle somewhat crestfallen. For as *ugly* as I am I think I am better looking than he is." There was no mention of Miss Connelly; despite his earlier protests, Arthur McKimmon's emotions had moved on.[56]

Some young men got quite caught up in the pursuit of romance. William Mullins of the University of North Carolina, for instance, expressed great excitement about commencement week because of the number of women who would be attending. In 1841 he wrote, "The cry is still they come and the Ladies are about to overrun the Hill. Every ten minutes a carriage comes and the fair creatures cluster thick around us on every side. Luck be with them! and more of them to share it!!" He had made a date to escort a young woman to chapel one of the mornings and he went to get her only "after giving my locks their proper air of graceful neglegé, and to my collar and neck-kerchief the most approved air." The day of the commencement, Mullins was like a fox in the henhouse with so many young ladies around. On his way to chapel, a fellow student stopped him "and insisted on my waiting on some of the young ladies, who had no beaux, to the chapel. This was certainly not a very irksome task, and I returned into the parlour with him, and was introduced to some three or four pretty girls, the prettiest of whom I immediately engaged for Chapel. I forget her name, but she looked very well, and I was very well pleased to take her up to the Halls, show her the pictures, and look around on the other pretty girls, (among whom were Misses H. & B. whose large dark lustrous eyes I several times caught beaming full upon me) until time to take her to Chapel."[57]

Students valued highly their physical attraction to potential sweethearts. In describing a temperance meeting he attended, Leonidas Siler told his cousin that he had flirted with twenty young ladies. He said that some were "right good looking," but most of them "were flat-nosed, redheaded, bumpy-faced and *big-footed.*" He said that he just could not muster the interest in any of these girls, especially since every time he tried, he thought of a girl back home. He rhapsodized, "Oh! what power has memory over us. I thought of happy days, blissful hours, o'erpowering moments, extatic scenes, heavenly looks, beautiful eyes,—times of innocent love & youthful courtship—and my own idol of perfection was again enthroned on the alter of my heart."[58]

The ideal of having a sweetheart and finding "the one" also captivated many of these maturing young men. Of course, physical attraction was important, but it was not necessary for everyone. Washington College student George Penn even became lovesick over the description of a young lady named Virginia Waldren, who had attended the Buckingham Female Collegiate Institute. "I had been told," he wrote to his sister, "she was quite handsome and an only child." He requested that his sister, also a Buckingham student, tell him whether she believed Miss Waldren to be "handsome and smart." He said that if he liked the description he would call and see her on his trip home. Penn's image of Miss Waldren was so favorable that he even attributed his "gloomy" feelings to the idea that he "must certainly be in love—with . . . the description I have had of Miss Waldren."[59]

In addition to the desires for love, many college students in the antebellum South entertained ideas of a more carnal nature. The southern code of honor held permissive attitudes toward male fornication. In fact, for men to repress their sexual impulses could even be seen as effeminate or prissy within that environment. Sexual conquest was an important rite of passage for male sons of the southern gentry. Southern parents tacitly supported this notion, believing that their boys should be prepared for marriage by being sexually experienced before their wedding night. According to Bertram Wyatt-Brown, with this level of expectation, young men of the South "made sexual experience a point of honor and boasting among themselves."[60]

As these young men sought sexual intercourse, however, they usually did not seek it from the "ladies" they pursued at social functions. At several colleges and universities students frequented prostitutes. In fact, one student at the University of Virginia reported that in 1840, when the enrollment at the university was only a few hundred, there were "80 cases of venereal disease" among them in one school session.[61]

Some students saw venereal disease as a mere inconvenience in their sexual exploits. South Carolina College student Thomas Jefferson

Withers recorded in a letter to a friend about feeling "horny," but he was afraid of getting the "clap." He had reasons for this fear, reporting that many of the "pale faces among the raking youth of the town evince its existence" and that because he had "past thro' the fiery furnaces of fear last June I feel as wild as a brick."[62] Similarly, when University of Virginia student D. B. DeSaussure wrote a letter to a classmate describing his summer, it contained references to numerous sexual encounters, including some in which he became infected with the "clap." He said that he spent time with another classmate, who supposedly knew "the ropes so well" when it came to intimate relations with women. DeSaussure reported that the young man's claims to have put "thro' nine women" had to be a lie, because "the very first thing he put me to over there clapped both of us." He felt fortunate that the "sulphur water" cured him in a few days. DeSaussure also reported that their classmate had "two of the biggest, fattest, bouncinest sisters in whole world."[63]

Upon leaving his friends, DeSaussure went to "the Springs," where many young ladies from around the South were spending their summer. There, he "got tight in the day & play'd billiards—or roll'd ten pins with the women, and at night waltzed & danced with the dear creatures." He added: "I was most interested in a mobile Girl—a Miss Foster— pretty—Rich—intelligent. we got on amazingly and on the third night I was allow'd the priviledge of calling her by an endearing name and promised to go on North with her next day & consum*mate* things in the fall at Mobile." His devotion to the young lady, however, was clearly not as serious as this account might seem. He did not go with the young lady, nor did he consummate anything, because, as he wrote, "Unfortunately I overslept myself next day or I w'd assuredly have gone."[64]

Other students went even farther than DeSaussure in their attitudes toward women. Charles Blackford and his friends at the University of Virginia formed an early version of the "He-Man Woman Hater's Club" that they called the "quadrangular coterie." The goals of this club included playing chess, eating oysters, and "reducing young women to their proper grade in society by demonstrating to the world around her that they are but human." He elaborated, stating that in the current age the fashion was to "exalt young females to a position little lower than the angels and to consider them an entirely distinct and superior order of creation." Blackford acknowledged that at some point his head might turn to the charms of a woman, but he had a plan. He expounded, "Well! my way is, if, when I have retired to my classic shade to study, a foul fiend whispers to my soul the charms of some far off beauty, I turn and read with renewed vigor Blackstone on 'marriage contracts'[;] if the same fell spirit suggests the charms of a domestic circle it just spins me to a more careful version of Kent on 'Husband & Wife' or 'Parent & Child.' Thus you see how women (young ones I mean) only make me the harder student."[65]

The idea of putting off love interests until the completion of studies was common. Many students enjoyed courtship but believed that marriage was to wait until they grew more mature and settled. In a series of letters to his cousin, University of North Carolina student Leonidas Siler confessed that he was romantically interested in a young woman from his hometown. But when answering the question of whether he "loved" her, he emphatically denied it, with the following explanation: "With regard to some other lady, whom you denominate my '*little angel,*' I of course have not determined on marrying her, even if I could get her, which I think very doubtful. She is good, kind, amiable and interesting; free from display and gives evidence of a firm, unwavering though unostentatious adherence to her beliefs and preference. But understand me; I am not in love nor do I desire to be until I shall have finished college. Then I will aid my friends in selecting me a wife."[66]

Even though some students expressed rather cavalier attitudes about marriage, this was not always the case. As students matured and approached graduation, their minds looked to the future. One Centenary College student addressed the issue of marriage in a public speech before his peers. He expressed a rather scathing criticism of his classmates and others his age for placing more value on fun and fashion than on thoughts of the future. He stated, in a quite serious manner: "Marry? Yes, marry. Who would not marry? Answer me, ye withered, soulless old bachelors, who stand like leafless, branchless, dead trees in the farmer's field; so deeply rooted in the stiff clay of life that ye stand erect; ye low and desolate trunks rifted by the winds, and dissolved by the rains of adverse fate. Answer this momentous question, ye self-styled lords of creation, whose ambition never soared higher than a high-heeled boot.

Ye pretenders with a golden chain in the vest hung to a trunk key in the pocket. And you, ye stricken daughters of leisure, who frisk and dance in the phosphorescent light of your genius, whose hearts are as hollow as an air bubble and your heads as soft as a frost-bitten pumpkin." In a stirring, and condemning climax, he passed judgment, stating, "Come! Come one, come all, and hear what is written against you: 'Beauty is but skin deep, ugly goes to the bone; Beauty soon fades away, but ugly holds its own.'"[67]

College life in the Old South was one of constant challenge and change. Students arrived at college as mere boys, but they had to function in an atmosphere that expected adult behavior. As they navigated the murky waters of college expectations, they also dealt with the vast ocean of life outside of the classroom. As they sought amusement and entertainment, they often did so with childlike expectations and intentions. After all, they had to behave as adults in the classroom, under the watchful eyes of the faculty. Nevertheless, these students were still on a journey to adulthood, and as they forged their college relationships, whether in a literary society or in search of a life mate, they helped themselves along that well-traveled path to maturity and acceptance in society at large.

Honor and Violence

RULES, PRANKS, RIOTS, GUNS, AND DUELS

I N 1851, one of the youthful students at South Carolina College stole the institution's bell from the college cupola. The perpetration of this prank would bring the students and faculty into a potentially perilous standoff in the world of honor. The bell's primary function at the college was to summon students to prayers and recitations. But in its absence, the students used their adolescent reasoning to assert that they no longer were required to attend prayers and recitations. The faculty found a replacement bell, but some students stated that only the original bell had the authority to bring them to classes. Other students made a more complicated case for ignoring the new bell: because the faculty had sent a servant to ring the chime, and by tradition, an officer of the college was supposed to be tasked with that duty, therefore, there was no authority in the action. Finally, the faculty met and decided that the defiance had gone on long enough, stating, "the students should attend the exercises at the legal hours, whether a bell was rung or not." The entire sophomore class, however, met and issued a resolution that they would not attend any exercise without the proper summons. Several freshmen and juniors joined in the resolution. The issue finally found solution when members of the trustees ordered that the replacement bell be hoisted into the college cupola before it was rung again. The next morning, with ringing resonating from the "official" home of the college bell, the standoff ended. "The effect was magical," wrote one professor, "the students gave prompt obedience, and the spirit of letters breathed upon all its gentle influence."[1]

A similar incident at Hampden-Sidney College in Virginia involved students reacting differently when faced with stern consequences to their actions. In the 1830s students there became angry at the college president when he refused to allow them to celebrate Washington's birthday in the nearby town of Kingsville. In retaliation, the students took the college bell from the president's gate, carried it away from the college, and buried it "with great ceremony." Upon discovering the theft, the president used the steward's tin horn to summon the students to their various classes and other exercises. Many refused to attend classes, with the excuse that they did not hear the bell. That evening, the president told them that "absence and tardiness in attendance on their College duties, arising from not hearing the bell, would not be excused by the Faculty," a condition that could result in expulsion. Many of the students still argued that the faculty should excuse their absences because of the missing bell. Two weeks later, when the president remarked that the faculty was reporting a large number of absences, the rebellious students realized that the president was serious in his threat. They held a meeting and thirty or forty of them "formed into a line and went in solemn order to the hiding place of the bell, and in an hour or more returned with it, and singing the most mournful songs. . . . The boys placed the bell in its original position on the form."[2]

Although both of these incidents may seem harmless, they reflected the existence of a student peer-developed honor ethic. College represented an important rite of passage during which students shed their past, having been surrounded by family and the familiar, and launched into a struggle for autonomy, self-governance, and interdependence within the adult world. The struggles that centered on these bell incidents typified many of the issues that guided this transitional period for them. Stealing the bell represented the students' adolescent immaturity, their continued connection to childhood. At South Carolina College the theft was for mere folly; at Hampden-Sidney it was in childish defense of what students perceived as their rights. The attempt to use the bells' absence as an excuse to avoid responsibilities was a furtherance of this immaturity. As the situation escalated, however, the students banded together in an honor-bound standoff with the faculty. At South Carolina College they mimicked the adult world around them, issuing their formal intentions in the language of honor: they would not be summoned by a replacement bell, rung by a mere servant, from a location other than the cupola. At Hampden-Sidney they simply ignored admonitions to return to class.

These actions thrust the students into the more complex adult world of antebellum social relations and expectations. The simple declaration of the faculty that the students should attend exercises, with or without the bell, was a direct challenge to their honor, and they would not back down. Instead, at South Carolina College it took a compromise from the adults—an arrangement to have the replacement bell rung from the cupola—before the students felt that their honor had been observed and they could once again attend class. On the other hand, at Hampden-Sidney, following through on a threat with consequences did the trick, illustrating the fact that these students were still boys in the grown-up world. What is clear in both situations is that either could have become violent at any turn as these adolescents tried to navigate the turbulent waters of adult honor.

As students in antebellum southern colleges worked out their relationships to the world of southern honor, they often had to face the challenges of debilitating rules and regulations. On the other hand, in the name of order, faculty and administrators believed it necessary to impose and enforce these rules. Such a combination could lead to violent confrontations.

An example of the difficulties southern colleges had with student conduct was reflected in the extensive rules and regulations published by the East Alabama Male College at its founding in 1859. Because the institution started so late in the antebellum period, it had the benefit of the accumulated experiences of faculty and administrators in older institutions of higher learning in the South. The college rules included a long list of "offenses" that would be "punished according to the degree of their aggravation": "Bringing or causing to be brought, spiritous liquor of any kind, within the town of Auburn, drinking intoxicating liquors, being concerned in any riot, making disturbances at night about the college, in the town of Auburn, or in any other place, striking a fellow student, association with any person of notoriously bad character, or with any student dismissed under censure, playing at cards or other gambling games, attending any ball, theatre, circus, horse-race, or cockfight, or any amusement forbidden by the Faculty, or to interrupt the exercises of the College, and doing any act, either singly or in concert with others, having a design or tendency to annoy the officers of the Faculty, or any of them or to obstruct them in the discharge of their duty." The college rules also gave specific punishment for some offenses: "Every person having in possession, either as his own property or as the property of another, a pistol or other deadly weapon, shall be at once dismissed from the College."[3]

Within an environment with these types of rules, adolescent behavior often came into conflict with the faculty's expectations. University of Alabama president Basil Manly II wrote often in his diary a chorus of complaints about student behavior in defiance of established rules. Manly's list of student misconduct during chapel services included: "whispering"; "using textbook in pr[ayers]"; "moving place and reading"; "scuffling before prayer"; "scuffle during roll call at pr[ayers]"; and "snapping at Capel as a dog." In another instance he recorded that a student had thrown firecrackers into the fire during a professor's lecture and that it had "made a report like that of a pistol." In yet another section, Manly complained: "The text books in Anct. Geography were nearly all taken from the freshmen class, & concealed.—addressed students & waited until Mon. Nov. 6. 9 O'clock. They were not returned." And then, three days later, he wrote, "It was either Foster (Fresh) or Ellis, or both that removed the text books, in anct. Geography. . . . I asked Foster about it, he neither confirmed nor denied it, but thought I c[oul]d not find out."[4]

Although these pranks ultimately proved harmless, their existence and the possibility of discovery and punishment always created the chance that the students' sense of honor would be disturbed. Manly related another incident in which this was the case. In 1844 he caught a student named Jarratt and others committing mischief in the gallery of the University Rotunda. The students had disguised themselves by wearing blackface, but Manly recognized Jarratt. The other students escaped. For students, behaving childishly was acceptable, as long as the adults, or "code-masters," did not discover them in their childish identity. Within two weeks of the incident, Jarratt was "so plagued by students about his being detected in disguise," wrote Manly, "that he availed himself of the plea of diarrhea . . . to write to his father, and to go home."[5]

In addition to the more general pranks perpetrated by students, such as hiding the college bell and making noise in common areas, some actions had more direct purposes, reflecting the occasional power struggles between the adolescent scholars and the adult faculty members. In explaining to Thomas Jones, an alumnus of the University of North Carolina, why his brother, John, had been suspended in 1814, faculty member Abner Stith gave an account from the perspective of the faculty and administration. He stated that some of the students had become offended with a faculty member and had formed an association dedicated to harassing him "as much as they could by committing depredations against his property." These students committed a variety of acts against the professor, including shaving his horse's tail and loosening his gate from its hinges and hiding it out of sight. The faculty, believing that the majority of students did not approve of these actions, questioned each student individually about his knowledge of the perpetrators. John Jones and a few others refused to answer any of the questions, so the administration assumed they were the guilty parties and turned to the civil courts. Every suspected student except John left the university rather than be summoned by the court. As a result, the faculty expelled all those who left; John received a four-month suspension. In explaining why those who did not talk were considered guilty, Stith simply stated: "I need not tell you the motives which necessitated them in withholding their information; for you having been a member of the College, know very well the customs of the students."[6]

In a similar incident at Virginia's Hampden-Sidney College, on July 21, 1805, several students "went on a rampage, ringing the college bell, placing pieces of lumber against the teacher's door to fall on him when he opened it, threw a brick through the window of the room of Mr. Crawford, a teacher, endangering the people in the room. The president and masters, and later the trustees, in trying to identify the culprits, met with considerable student resistance in their efforts." In the end the board suspended the entire student body, except six who agreed to testify, until it met again on July 29. At the July 29 meeting, three students were expelled for their continued refusal to testify. Two others refused to talk and received suspension with the possibility of readmittance only with "satisfactory evidence of contrition to the president and the teachers." Five students finally admitted their involvement in the destruction and received one-month suspensions.[7]

Problems also erupted into violence between students and faculty at the University of Virginia in 1825—its first year. The university's founder, Thomas Jefferson, declared that "vicious irregularities" were occurring among the students in their behavior. These behavioral difficulties were based on anti-foreign sentiment regarding the university professors. Several students masked themselves and gathered on the Lawn one night, chanting, "Down with the European professors!" Two of the faculty came to investigate the noise, and one of them grabbed a student, whereupon other students threw bricks at him and beat his colleague with a cane. The next day, sixty-five students signed a petition against the two professors for "daring to lay hands" on a student. After this incident the faculty demanded effective policing and threatened to resign if something were not done to quell student unrest. At Jefferson's recommendation, the board of visitors drew up a restrictive code, which included a strict bedtime of 9:00 P.M., a requirement to rise at dawn, and "an officially prescribed dull gray uniform." In addition, the board outlawed drinking, gambling, and smoking, and they required all students to deposit all of their money with the university proctor. Finally, the board expelled those students most heavily involved in the riot.[8]

As students navigated their place in the adult world away from home, their attempts to enjoy the freedoms of independence also led to conflict with the faculty and administrators. In the world of honor, students felt compelled to prepare their public faces—their masks as southern gentlemen—as they interacted with the world around them. This activity, however, often brought more restrictive rules and caused discord in the college community. In 1850, for instance, the junior class at South Carolina College rebelled against the institution. One of the professors had fallen ill, prompting the president to appoint another teacher to instruct the class. The students, however, contended that they no longer had to attend the class, leading to a face-off of wills. As the events moved into riotous behavior, the president acted decisively: he suspended sixty students, breaking up the junior class.[9]

In a similar action in February 1845, the University of Virginia faculty suspended three members of a student musical group which called itself the Callathumpians for causing a disturbance. Swift to retaliate, the Callathumpians threw sticks and stones at the faculty chairman's house, but some were caught and suspended. The conflict entered a dormant stage in which all thought the affair had ended, but in April Callathumpians went to one of the professors' houses in the middle of the night with drums and horns, causing quite a bit of noise. They then threw rocks at his windows, but were surprised when the professor emerged from the darkness and captured one of the students, threatening to shoot anyone who came to the boy's aid. This action caused an escalation. Over the next several nights, students staged assaults of rocks and other projectiles on faculty houses and rode horses through the campus while firing pistols in the air. Finally, the faculty called in the civil authorities to restore order.

Most of the students had not been involved in the rioting and were quite distressed to hear that the militia was to be called to campus. A student petition declared that if they were left to handle the situation, the rioting would come to an end. Twenty of the ringleaders had left the campus, and the students believed the matter was resolved already. Nevertheless, the faculty invited the militia anyway, leaving the students indignant and feeling that the honor of their word had been ignored. A new student petition denounced the faculty and accused them of causing the riots. Of the 194 students enrolled at the University of Virginia, 106 joined the 20 ringleaders and withdrew in protest over this affair.[10]

Another cause of discord on southern campuses came when students lived beyond their immediate means, attracting the wrath of local merchants to whom they owed money. This proved to be a particular problem at the University of Alabama in the 1830s. In 1835, A. L. Pickens wrote to his guardian that he and his cousin, both students at the university, had acquired a large debt in Tuscaloosa. He wrote: "In dissolving some of our accounts—those which remain unpaid will amount to nearly $300." Pickens's solution was typical. He asked that his guardian send that amount with an additional hundred dollars for board "as soon as possible."[11]

With the potential for increasing friction between the university community and the citizens of Tuscaloosa, the faculty urged the creation of a more restrictive merit and demerit system to better control student behavior. In 1836, these new rules sparked a series of violent riots by the students, which shook "the public confidence in the university and brought on its temporary decline." The system to which the students objected so strongly preyed on their honor. It held students accountable in a public manner for their failings at school. The system required that periodic statements be sent to the parents "from which they will be able to form an accurate opinion of the progress made by their sons in their education; of their attention to their daily collegiate exercises; and of their general moral deportment." What was particularly irksome for the students, but a brilliant stroke by a faculty who understood the power of the honor ethic, was the fact that the academic standing of the students was "made . . . public at the University, and consequently obtains partial publicity in the neighboring community." A committee charged with investigating the catalyst of these riots judged that the merit/demerit system partially caused the outbreak, but they expressed their approval of the public nature of the plan. They wrote: "The system itself, happily combines the principles which operate on the pride and fears of the students, and powerfully excites and brings into action that noble and virtuous emulation which stimulates distinction in his literary attainments, and to pursue with diligence and industry, his college studies."[12]

This committee also offered other insights into why the students were "ripe for rebellion." It first asserted that any rule that "might interfere with their pleasures, or require strict attention to duties, would probably have been seized upon as a pretext for the outrages they committed." But beyond this charge, the committee also believed that parental laxity was the first culprit for these privileged youths. They blamed parents for sending their sons to college with the means of "supplying themselves with every thing which extravagance or vices of the times, have brought into use." They continued: "It is too common with parents, to give their sons extensive, and often, unlimited credit in Tuskaloosa, and to furnish them with considerable sums of money, which their wants and comforts do not require. Prone, as young men are, to participate in the pleasures and amusements of what is denominated fashionable life, and to plunge into its excesses too, it is not to be wondered at, that thus supplied, they neglect their studies, and become impatient at the restraints and discipline of the University." As evidence, the committee pointed out that many young men considered going to the university as "entering on a theatre where they are to appear as men of the world." As a result, the students arrive having bought "costly and extravagant wardrobes, liberal supplies from the best jewelry establishments, and then the indispensible appendages of dirks, pistols, Bowie knives, &c." The committee concluded that unless the students abandoned "all idea of becoming conspicuous and fashionable gentlemen before they are educated boys—they had better remain at home; for it is vain and useless to hope that they will ever become scholars, or realise the anxious expectations of their parents."[13]

Just as the committee indicated, violence on southern campuses occasionally escalated because of the presence of weapons among students. Many colleges and universities had to pass specific rules forbidding students from possessing deadly weapons while at school. Just after the 1805 "student rampage" at Hampden-Sidney, for instance, the board of trustees used the incident as the catalyst to vote in a new regulation against anyone on the campus either keeping or shooting pistols.

At the University of North Carolina, the mixture of alcohol and firearms in the southern environment proved bloody in 1845. One evening, several students from the university headed to a local tavern in the town of Hillsboro. According to one of their classmates, these students were "the rowdy kind." While at the tavern, one of the students "fell in with some loafers and got drunk." The tavern keeper tried to get them to quiet down, and raised a chair threateningly at one of the loafers. In reaction, the drunken student produced a pistol from his coat and fired it, wounding the man in the arm. The student "fled immediately from the state." His actions, however, reflected an ethic drummed into him in the southern culture. According to his classmates, the young man had frequently been heard to say that his father always told him "to shoot any person, if he had any difficulty with him."[14]

In the gun-toting southern society, for students to possess firearms represented a connection to the adult world. As a result, many students owned and carried guns, despite strict rules banning such actions. They even felt great satisfaction when they were able to conceal their weapons from the faculty. In 1841, University of North Carolina student William Sydney Mullins demonstrated this elation when he explained that at the beginning of every session the college president would visit each student's room and "enquire of the occupants if they have any guns, pistols, or other deadly weapons." When the president came to Mullins's room and asked the question, Mullins's roommate, described as "one of the stoutest fellows in College," replied by shaking his fist in the air and saying, "None but this, sir." The president "laughed heartily" at the reply and then moved on. To Mullins's delight, he was able to report to his friends: "I had a pistol in the draw[er] and therefore said nothing, but let Tom talk."[15]

With the presence of firearms on southern campuses, accidents occurred. In November 1842, a group of Washington College students had gone "possum hunting" with pistols. When they returned without any luck, they decided to shoot their weapons at targets instead. One student named Gamble pulled the trigger, exploding the percussion cap, but not firing the pistol. When he returned the gun to his pocket, it discharged, firing into his leg. According to one student, news of the accident spread through the college "with the rapidity of electricity" and most students and faculty rushed to the young man's aid. Gamble convalesced in a private home and eventually returned to the college, but the doctor was not able to remove the ball from his thigh.[16]

Perhaps the most notorious antebellum example of college student adolescent behavior, the adult code of honor, and the presence of firearms came from the University of Virginia in 1840. Even with the most serious of outcomes—the murder of a professor—students still believed that they had the right to dispense justice to the perpetrator. In November, several masked students were firing blank pistol cartridges into the night air when word came that Professor A. G. Davis was on his way to stop them. One of the students loaded his weapon with powder and ball and waited for a confrontation. As Davis approached, he tried to remove the student's mask; the student shot him in the abdomen. Davis died several hours later.

Other students expressed their absolute horror with the tragic outcome of the night's events. One of them, Robert Dabney, asserted: "The students have almost unanimously evinced the most praiseworthy sympathy, and the greatest desire to bring the offenders to justice." Insisting that they be the ones to apprehend the murderer, they created search parties and had the guilty student under arrest by the next day. They believed that honor dictated their actions, and expressed pride in their very adult behavior after this incident. According to Dabney, "At first, the students had everything to do. The faculty & the authorities seemed tacitly to give up matters into our hands. Indeed they could have done nothing without us, for the constables & sheriffs are all afraid to apprehend the students, and they left all that work to us. If the students had not taken the matter into their own hands, the rascals might have run to never, before the lazy town folks fairly got their eyes open. Our conduct is every where well spoken of, where it is understood."[17]

Violence between students represented another significant area of tumult on southern campuses. The severity of the aggression varied, but because these students were adolescents, the potential for escalation always loomed over them. Although outlawed, duels often settled conflicts of honor in southern society. On a college campus, therefore, an adolescent fistfight could soon escalate into mortal combat. The volatility of student interactions created an atmosphere in which students had to guard their behavior with the knowledge that their actions might produce deadly results. Occasionally, however, students forgot this truism of southern life, resulting in direct conflict with their peers.

Any perceived insult could be the catalyst for violent confrontation. On January 25, 1848, University of Alabama student Edward Baptist was due to give a recitation in class, so he practiced in his room, determined to please his professor. But a childish prank perpetrated on him that day—and his reactions to it—would change his life forever. While Baptist prepared in his room, his friend, James T. Killough, mischievously locked the door from the outside. Upon discovery of the prank, and anxious not to be late to the recitation, Baptist broke the lock and angrily brushed by Killough, who stood laughing outside the door. When Baptist returned, Killough confronted him, asking why Baptist had pushed by him so brusquely. Still angry, Baptist replied that he intended to have no further communication with Killough, who responded by calling Baptist a "damned rascal." Insulted, Baptist then directed a friend to issue a "challenge" to Killough to fight. Killough believed he was being challenged to a duel, meaning he would get to choose the conditions. Killough announced that they would fight naked, armed with Bowie knives. Baptist, therefore, found himself in the midst of a dilemma: he had only intended a fistfight, but the southern honor ethic that guided his society dictated that if he backed down from this deadly path he would be branded a coward—a label that could follow him the rest of his life.[18]

The struggle that confronted Baptist and Killough typified many of the issues that guided this transitional period for them. Killough's prank represented his adolescent immaturity, his continued connection to childhood. Baptist's rebuff of the prank, however, reflected a more adultlike response, propelling the two into the more complex adult world of antebellum social relations and expectations. The honor ethic among adult white males in the South demanded that Baptist obtain "satisfaction" for being labeled a "damned rascal." When Baptist issued his challenge, however, he too was still dwelling in the world of the child, expecting an adolescent fistfight. Killough had moved beyond that. He demanded an "adult" duel, using Bowie knives, and fighting naked to prevent the possibility of concealing additional weapons. Baptist was left with a difficult decision—should he leave the world of the child once and for all and agree to the duel with Killough? Should he back down and risk being branded a man without honor by his classmates? Ultimately, Baptist sought the guidance of the university's president, Basil Manly. Understanding the full implications of the decision, Manly suggested that Baptist should leave the university rather than face the bitter ridicule of his classmates. Baptist took this advice.[19]

Of course, because these students were adolescents, fistfights did occur without escalation to anything more. Knowing the dangers, faculty generally reacted quickly to intervene—usually through suspending the participants from school. In 1823, University of North Carolina student F. W. Harrison reflected on this course of action, writing: "There took place the other day a suspension of two of the members of my class, for the fact of fighting, which is rather too prevalent in College and ought to be suppressed by some exessive means."[20] Nevertheless, when student conflict did escalate, many students believed that their peers had gone too far into the adult world. Robert Dabney at Hampden-Sidney reported in 1837 that one of his classmates had received suspension for issuing a challenge for a duel to one of his fellows. Although he concluded that "no evil consequences are likely to result from it," he further editorialized that the "affair happened between two mere boys, who ought to have fought it out with birches."[21]

Contrary to Dabney's opinion, southern students often found themselves locked in deadly combat. In September 1841, University of North Carolina student James L. Dusenbery wrote about a fight between two students, Bunch and Rice. Bunch had insulted Rice during a meeting of the Philanthropic Literary Society, and the two met to fight the next morning. Dusenbery reported that Bunch was universally despised and considered a "rascal." Bunch had few friends to support him. During the fight, Rice knocked Bunch to the ground, then Bunch grabbed a pistol and fired, missing Rice, but hitting Rice's older brother in the hip. Dusenbery asserted that Rice then grabbed a large stick, and Rice's friends would not allow Bunch to have a stick since he had fired the pistol. He continued, "They fought thus unequally for several minutes & Bunch was well nigh beaten to a mummy." Both combatants received expulsion for the fight, and Rice's brother was not wounded seriously.[22]

Another catalyst for unrest between students was the age-old quest to attract members of the opposite sex. Student courtship rituals often involved competition and even violence. On February 22, 1861, students at the University of Mississippi held a ball. At the party, two students expressed interest in one young lady, but she returned her attentions to only one of them. The two men exchanged sharp words on the ballroom floor, and the rejected student threatened to meet the other later that night. Both were armed and both had classmates supporting their positions. After escorting the young lady to her home, the successful student was returning to the campus with a group of his friends when he discovered his opponent waiting for him with a crowd. The two mobs pushed the students together, and the rejected suitor struck his rival. The other student immediately pulled out a pistol, wounded his attacker, and then returned to the university. The gunman went to court three days later, and the shooting was ruled justifiable. Both students then appeared before a faculty hearing and the wounded student was expelled, while the shooter was advised to withdraw from the university.[23]

Even with the normal swift expulsion of combatants, fights did not always lead to punishment, even when observed by faculty members. In 1846, a University of Alabama professor saw A. B. Brumby attack fellow student William W. Martin. Neither participant suffered reprimand for this violation because of the circumstances and outcome. Brumby, who was described as a "little runt," had been "poking fun & ridicule at Martin," who was described as "a half-witted fellow" but "stout & strong." Fed up with the ridicule, Martin took the smaller Brumby to task and Brumby charged him. According to witnesses, "Martin did not attempt to hit or strike Brumby—who merely seized Martin and was tugging about his middle—scarcely able to reach higher, and unable to do any damage." He concluded, "It was a sort of comical affair."[24]

Even "comical" events, however, could lead students into uncharted waters of potential combat. In 1840, University of North Carolina student William Mullins and some of his classmates decided to engineer a hoax on several students at the college by staging a quarrel between Mullins and another student. Mullins then publicly challenged the other student to a duel. He wrote that "On Monday the whole West Building became acquainted with the circumstances and several of the Fresh were frightened to death. On Tuesday the excitement continued unabated there, but on Wednesday, it rather flagged as rumors of a hoax began to grow rife, and we burst the bubble ourselves. . . . Several of the students . . . were hoaxed bad and on the whole, the humbug, though not equal to our intentions, was partially successful." After reflecting on the whole affair, Mullins offered, "It has taught me several important lessons. In the first place, unnecessary delay is fatal to a hoax. The meeting between us should have taken place on Monday and I urged on them that, it should, but was overruled. In the next place, the most consummate caution must be used. We were not sufficiently prudent." He concluded that the most important lesson he learned, however, was "*never to engage in such an affair again. They* can do no good—they *may* do much harm. Those who are hoaxed are apt to be offended: and those not, raise a laugh that is rather annoying. They do not produce a favourable impression of an individual's steadiness or gravity and are well adapted to diminish respect."[25]

Unfortunately for Mullins, his fears about diminished respect proved prophetic; within three weeks some of his classmates had taken to derisively hailing him the "Hero of the Sham Duel." Mullins took offense and vowed that if he heard the sobriquet again, he would publicly curse the speaker, adding, "and if he attacks me, his blood be on his own head." Mullins was so offended by the criticism that he believed that his honor had been challenged. He wrote: "if they force me to an encounter, I shall not shrink from carrying it to extremes, even if it involves one of their lives. I will endeavour to teach certain individuals that it is not as easy to put down a student, as they may think. That this is their design, I am convinced, and I am forced in self-defense to carry the war into Africa." With a dramatic flair, he added, "On the result perhaps depends my destiny."

Three days later, Mullins received a letter from fellow student P. P. Spencer, who owed Mullins money and cigars in payment for a wager. Spencer addressed the letter to "Mr. Philo Whist alias The Champion of the Sham Duel." Mullins first tried to challenge Spencer to a duel, but decided to send a letter instead, in which he stated: "Mr. Mullins regrets the necessity of holding any correspondence with Mr. P. P. Spencer . . . and he cannot condescend from his dignity as a gentleman to bandy epithets; he can only say that he does not consider the individual to whom this note is addressed as a gentleman." He concluded that he was pleased to hear that he would be receiving the money and cigars owed him because he "never expected to get it." Mullins speculated that as a result of this note Spencer would either challenge him or publicly attack him. He wrote: "If he does the first, I will accept it; if he attempts the last, I have arms and shall do my duty to myself. I shall bear a pistol constantly with me: if necessary, I know how to use it." Spencer did neither, and the "hero of the Sham Duel" never actually had to fight to defend his honor. He went on with his college career without engaging in any more potentially inflammable adolescent behaviors.[26]

The presence of violence in antebellum southern colleges, perhaps more than anything else, confirms that students there lived in a dual world. Their behavior clearly reflected that of adolescents, who were in the process of navigating the chasm between childhood and adulthood. But adolescence could not explain all of their actions. The existence of the honor ethic injected a formative structural element into the developmental process. As they yearned to act and behave as adults, their under-standing of southern honor would push them into potentially harmful conflict. Whether uniting to protest what they saw as a faculty slight, or engaging in mortal combat with their peers, college students often erupted with violence. This reality planted them firmly in the world of the Old South, and helped them define who they were.

CHAPTER 5

College Life and the Civil War

THE AMERICAN CIVIL WAR substantively changed college life in the Old South more than any other single event in American history. Collegiate existence, as the sons and daughters of the southern elite had come to know it, came to an end. The war brought confusion, division, and, ultimately, resolve to college students, but in the process it tore apart the delicate threads of antebellum southern social relations.

As the war approached, the first waves of discord could be seen in a series of incidents at Washington College in Lexington, Virginia, in late 1860 and early 1861. Abraham Lincoln's election to the presidency divided students there on the issue of secession, as it did the faculty. President George Junkin was an ardent unionist and tried to quell any support for secession. But seven students, including H. Rutherford Morrison, son of one of the college's trustees, caused an uproar when on December 10, 1860, they hoisted a secession flag over the college under the cover of night. Morrison described the flag as "blue with one blood red star in the middle and DISUNION painted in large letters above it." He further asserted that some students had threatened to pull down the flag immediately, "but we told them that if they tried there would be a war." In relating this incident, another student noted the sad irony that such a flag would be "raised on the roof of the college endowed by the father of his country, yea; even over his head." He further reported that "the sight of the flag the next morning fairly made Dr. Junkin pale with rage, he threatened to cane the traitorous fellow if he could find him."[1]

President Junkin ordered the flag removed, but the secession students had anticipated this action and had hidden all ladders at the college. President Junkin arranged for a ladder to be brought from town, but heavy winds thwarted any attempt to remove the flag for the rest of the day. That night, secession students guarded the banner against removal by pro-union students. When the flag finally came down the next day, Junkin ordered it to be burned and invited prominent townspeople to be present for the incineration. The secession students, however, were able to steal the flag from the president's room before it could be destroyed, launching Junkin into an enraged search of all student rooms to find the banner. He never did.

Junkin continued to fight his crusade against secession. He lectured against it in the classroom, using constitutional and moral arguments. But fewer and fewer students listened, and some labeled him a "Pennsylvania Abolitionist." Junkin also found scrawled on a column next to his recitation room the words "Lincoln Junkin." Through March, further flag incidents occurred and Junkin met each one with a rising fury. He even had another confiscated flag stolen from his room. So, in early April, when yet another secession banner appeared and Junkin had it pulled down, several students standing near him asked what he intended to do. Junkin produced some matches, set the banner ablaze, and exclaimed: "So *perish* all efforts to dissolve this glorious Union!" Students then tore off strips of the burned flag and, in defiant protest of their president's actions, wore them as insignia on their clothing.

Upon the news of Fort Sumter's surrender, Lincoln's call for troops, and Virginia's secession vote, students raised yet another flag. But this time things had changed: most of the faculty had now begun to side with the secessionists. Junkin once again insisted that the flag be removed, but a professor handed him a student petition to read before taking any action. The document stated: "It being our unanimous opinion that we, as a portion of the young men of Virginia, should signify our approbation of the recent action of our State Convention, and our willingness, if need be, to sustain the same in the trying scenes that may ensue, we have hoisted a southern flag over the College, as the best exponent of our views. It is now our unanimous desire, that the flag should continue to float; and we, therefore, respectfully request, that you will not suffer it to be taken down." Considering that abolitionist John Brown had only recently been executed for "treason against Virginia," the petition added ominously that there "can be no opposition to it from any quarter *now,* save from the enemies of Virginia, and we know that the people of this vicinity are loyal to the old Mother State, and they have no desire to interfere with it."

Junkin considered the flag to be a personal insult and announced to the faculty that he would leave the decision up to them. He also stated that he would not give another lecture until the flag came down, and that if the faculty did not vote to remove it, they would have his immediate resignation. Junkin resigned a day later following a faculty vote to support the students. He left for Pennsylvania soon thereafter.[2]

The students at Washington College reflected the emotions felt by college students throughout the South at the beginning of this war. Some reacted quickly in the name of rebellion, while others remained on the sidelines, waiting to see what would happen. With faculty often from the North, the situation grew tense as the days crept by. Nevertheless, college life did continue, but it was a life full of adjustments, confusion, difficulties, resolve, and survival.

As the political climate heated up in the months before the war, college students expressed a variety of opinions. Both the young men and women of southern institutions wanted to feel a part of the growing debate. Andrew McCollam, at Louisiana's Centenary College, reported in the month before Lincoln's election that the "subject of politics is very much discussed here at present, every street corner is the scene of an animated discussion on the issue of political parties, and on every side the ear is greeted with the harangues of embryo politicians." He asserted that the majority of students supported "Bell & Everett" for the presidential ticket, but that people of the town were more in favor of "Brecenridge & Lane."[3]

But six weeks later, McCollam learned with the rest of Louisiana that Abraham Lincoln had won the executive office. His reaction was one of confusion and fear. He wrote to his father for news, asking about the people of his home parish: "How do the people take Lincoln's election? inclined to submit or not?" He then editorialized that the "country is in a sad condition indeed, and if the 'signs of the times' may be relied upon in the estimate of probabilities, we must come to the conclusion that the Union of the states is doomed." McCollam tried to put the "impending crisis" into historical perspective, stating that at other periods in the American past "we have been surrounded by danger so emminent that the most sanguine gave up all as lost, but in the stormiest hour some bold spirit has arisen in the councils of the nation, to seize the helm, and soothe those discordant elements which threatened national ruin. But in our present perill," he continued, "we have no one to look to for assistance, passion and prejudice are to be our only guides, and much as we may hope to the contrary, reason tells us that the inevitable tendency of affairs is towards disunion." He concluded with a sense of resignation to the nation's plight: "I had hoped to live out the time I shall have on earth beneath the laws, and under the protection of that government which was modeled by the hands of our early patriots, and sustained by their arms during our collonial strugle; but I fear that it has been ordered otherwise."[4]

Regional differences even within the South also found their way into attitudes about the "impending crisis." In writing to a girlfriend in his home state of South Carolina in November of 1860, University of Virginia student George K. Miller expressed frustration with Virginians in their hope for compromise in the southern conflict with the Union. Miller asserted that he was "an uncompromising secessionist" and that he felt "truly proud that I am a South Carolinian . . . [and] hope she will be the first to secede for I believe it is a part of honour firstly due her." He further asserted that if South Carolina did secede and the Federal government used force to coerce the state back into the Union, he would "be there in two days" to defend it. He also reported that at the University of Virginia "most of the Carolina and Alabama students have donned the blue cockade"—a sign of southern solidarity and defiance of the Union. Miller was such an ardent secessionist, however, that he refused to wear the badge because he had learned that they had been "made by special order in a northern city." The girlfriend to whom he had written his letter, however, sent him a handmade blue cockade from his home state within the next two weeks. He wrote that when he wore it, he was the envy of the other students who favored secession. Some even asked him to divide the badge with them "when they heard it was all the way from So. Carolina & from one of its fair daughters."[5] Within a world of honor defined by one's public face, young Miller played the part well.

Not all students, however, reacted with such fervor about the coming conflict. Indeed, it must be remembered that these young scholars were still adolescents who often viewed the world around them in terms of their own lives and problems. Upon hearing of Lincoln's election, a freshman at Virginia's Hampden-Sidney College was heard speaking to an excited crowd of his classmates. "Fellow students," he stated, "it will be a glorious thing if the war does come, for then we will not have to stand those six books of Geometry." Evidently his fellow students greeted his reasoning favorably.[6]

Despite this type of cavalier attitude, the move toward secession in the southern states affected these young people directly. When it came, many colleges and universities in the South ceased to exist because the young men all left for the battlefield. With the opening cannon blasts at Fort Sumter, many southern students were swept up in the martial spirit moving through the South. In late April 1861, University of Virginia student Walter C. Preston wrote about this feeling in a letter to his father. "We are anxious to leave here and have a fight with Gen Scotts collection from Yankeedom, Ireland, France, Spain, Germany &c.," he asserted. The reason for this eagerness was to prove they were men of honor in the southern tradition. He elaborated that they wanted to go "just merely to show that we boys are not afraid to shed our blood, or get a scratch or so for the honor of the Old Dominion." His sense of pride in his fellow Virginians also produced a level of arrogance about their chances. He opined, "We expect, or at least I do, that we will have to fight a good many battles, but not hard ones; as yankees consider man's first duty to be, taking care of himself; & they will in all probability find the cheapest and surest way to find that desirable end—self preservation—when an army of Virginians come to the charge, is to drop their arms and get out of the way as fast as possible."[7]

In addition to sentiments of pride and honor, southern college students also departed out of a sense of duty. When Andrew McCollam of Centenary learned of the Union preparations for putting down the rebellion, he expressed concern about the Confederacy's ability to field a sizable, well-equipped army. He told his father that he planned to join a local company being organized to meet the threat, because "it is clearly and unmistakably my duty to do so." He argued that it was "a time of fearful danger to the confederacy and every one able to bear a musket should sacrifice personal considerations to the safety of the country." He concluded that a final reason for his enlistment was that "those who have no families depending on them should be the first to take the field."[8]

McCollam was not alone in his sentiments. Young men at colleges and universities throughout the South dropped their books and picked up their muskets. East Alabama Male College student Frank Little explained that his institution closed in 1861 because all of the students had left for war, "with well nigh all the College student body of the South."[9] McCollam's Centenary College suffered the same fate, unable to continue operations after the spring 1861 term. The faculty had intended to open the doors again that fall, but the October 7, 1861, notation in the faculty minute book explained with thirteen simple words why they could not: "Students have all gone to war. College suspended. and God help the right!"[10]

Another factor in drawing students from the ranks of collegiate enrollments was the implementation of a military draft in the Confederacy. The southern congress passed the first conscription law on April 16, 1862, requiring military service from all white men between the ages of eighteen and thirty-five. For many colleges that had survived intact through the first wave of patriotic enlistments, this law would wipe them out. By May 1862, for instance, all but five students at Wake Forest had succumbed to the draft, forcing the college to close its doors for the duration of the war.[11]

Some colleges fought hard to stay alive in the face of conscription. With the draft age beginning at eighteen, Dr. Daniel Bittle, president of Virginia's Roanoke College, saw that most students who were seventeen did not enroll because they knew that on their eighteenth birthday they would be forced to leave to enter the army. He went to Richmond to discuss the matter with Confederate authorities. The Secretary of War granted permission for any student who might arrive at military age in the middle of a school term to stay until the end of that session. This provision helped Roanoke recruit students. There were conditions, however, imposed by the Confederate officials: All students "of 16 years and upwards should have guns, furnished by the government, and pass through a regular military drill once a week; and that whenever raids were threatened upon Roanoke county, or upon the adjoining portions of Virginia, this company was to leave the institution and assist in repelling the enemy."[12]

Colleges and universities throughout the South that managed to remain open often did so by transforming themselves into military officer training institutions. Cadet corps sprung up on campuses throughout the region. The University of Virginia, for example, reorganized into such a structure in early 1861. By April, one student reported to his family that the university had "become little more than a military school." He informed them that they had formed three military companies on campus. He explained: "We drill on the Lawn in front of the Rotunda, an hour & a quarter every evening, so that there can be seen th[r]ee companies there every day now." He added with pride that "Two hundred and forty men will not make a poor show for the University."[13]

Being in the cadet corps was important for students who had not yet followed their peers into battle. It gave them a sense that they were part of the larger war effort. It also allowed them to feel a part of the adult world. The frivolity of youth was giving way rapidly to the seriousness of being an adult. Military drill instilled confidence in the young scholars. One University of Alabama cadet even felt so sure of himself that when he learned that his father was enlisting to fight, the boy sent advice about the soldiering life. Drawing on his mere weeks of experience performing military drill at the university, the boy wrote to his sister: "Tell Pa that when he is in ranks he must keek [keep] eyes to the Front, Chin drawn in and hands down and he will make a good soldier."[14]

The transition to a military regime on southern campuses, however, was not always a smooth one. In November 1860, Hampden-Sidney College formed a military corps and ran into immediate organizational difficulties. One of their first attempts at drilling became a comical affair. A contemporary described the scene as follows: "As we came upon the 'campus,' our attention was directed to a 'malicious' company of individuals, whose ferocious looks betokened the sterness of their purpose. Capt. P— was endeavoring to initiate their pliant minds into the mysteries of the 'science.' . . . 'Right flank, right face,' the company turns to the left. 'Wheel,' a third obeyed, another third went wrong while the balance looked astonished." After further unsuccessful commands, the company quit for the day, but according to the witness, the "general orders for the next day were, meet after chapel, call 'hem' for half an hour, to acquire the proper pitch of voice, and march to victory or to Booker's [the Steward's Hall, where they ate their meals]."

A few months later, Hampden-Sidney's company reorganized with the help of the college president, but this move did not guarantee success. President John M. P. Atkinson had no military training whatsoever, yet he became the drill captain. His presence in command of the squad insured that parents supported their sons' joining the company, but it did not assure any success. President Atkinson was so unsure of himself that he chose to drill the students at night in the basement of one of the buildings to avoid the criticism of onlookers. One of the cadets recalled his command style, reporting: "When he undertook to induct us into the mysteries of the 'double quick,' he commenced his explanation by saying: 'Gentlemen, when I count one, you will bring up the right foot until the thigh is perpendicular to the body, and when I count two, you will bring the other up beside it.'"[15] This was not exactly a model designed to instill military proficiency.

Most schools that changed to a military model did so because of the war—but not all. The University of Alabama made the switch before the war for completely different reasons. When Landon C. Garland became president of that university in 1855, he believed that the school's reputation had suffered too long from a lack of discipline. He decided that the only answer was to turn the institution into a military college, structured along the lines of the Citadel, the Virginia Military Institute, and the Military Academy at West Point. In 1860, the state legislature and the university board of trustees approved the plan, and by the fall session the school had been transformed. Students were now officially the Alabama Corps of Cadets, a component of Alabama's state troops. They had to wear uniforms and then began their session with four weeks of military drill before their classes even commenced. These actions worked. Students who had flouted all rules in the past and who had challenged authority at every turn were now bowing to the military regulations as a matter of course. Hard study and discipline replaced the drunkenness and gambling that had been the hallmarks of the old university.[16]

Of course, with war raging, forming university cadet corps meant that the students would probably see combat. Being able to drill with their adolescent peers provided a source of strength and courage for these students. Centenary's Andrew McCollam wrote to his mother in January 1861 that he had joined the college's military company and that he found it "a very amusing as well as profitable manner of spending Saturday morning; our Captain & First Lieutenant will go down to Baton Rouge on tomorrow to procure rifles for the Company." He further explained that the company could be ordered into active service "only in cases of emminent danger to the state, such as the approach of an invading army, or in case of a servile insurrection." In either case, he assured his mother that she would be able to refer to her son as "your 'most dutifull' being on the march for the 'tented field.'"[17]

The march to the tented field happened quickly for some student-cadets. In December 1860, students at the University of Mississippi had formed a military company—the University Greys. In late February 1861 they were mustered in as state troops and received weapons and supplies from the state government. The boys had the support of the town of Oxford, where the ladies performed a concert to raise funds to purchase a banner for them. By late April, the University Greys were mustered into Confederate service, and they departed the university on May 1, 1861. Those students who had not joined the Greys also left, and the university president wrote the next day, "We are indeed inhabitants of a solitude. Our University has ceased to have visible existence. Its halls are completely deserted, and its officers are without occupation."[18]

The Hampden-Sidney College drill company also found its way into combat. Months after its initial bungling formation, the company had improved significantly, and its members adopted the name "Hampden-Sidney Boys." They donned Confederate gray uniforms and put "H.S.B." in gilt on the brim of their caps. In May 1861, they were called into active service and mustered in as Company G of the 20th Virginia Regiment. Their history as a company is short; the Federal army captured the Hampden-Sidney Boys in July 1861 at the Battle of Rich Mountain. Detained in Beverly, Virginia, the college boys had few troubles as prisoners for several reasons. First, their captain was the college president, John M. P. Atkinson, a Presbyterian minister. He led prayer services for both the Confederate prisoners and their Federal captors. Second, several of the northern soldiers were also college students and they learned that many of the Hampden-Sidney men were in the same fraternities, so they "made their stay very pleasant and comfortable," remembered one student-soldier. Third, Gen. George B. McClellan took a particular interest in the Hampden-Sidney students and came to see them. He told them they should get back to their books at college and promised them they would see their mothers very soon. He was true to his word. The Hampden-Sidney company was paroled only six days after the battle. The students did not get officially exchanged for more than a year, and therefore, they remained at college until August 1862. When their exchanges did come through, the company never reformed; those who wanted to fight went home and joined their local units.[19]

The cadets from the Virginia Military Institute found themselves in combat as well. As Union troops under the command of Gen. Franz Sigel descended upon the vital Shenandoah Valley, on May 10, 1864, Confederate major general John C. Breckinridge sent an urgent dispatch to the V.M.I. superintendent, Francis Smith, asking for reinforcements from the Institute's Corps of Cadets. A battalion of four infantry companies and a section of artillery, totaling 247 cadets, set out immediately to join Breckinridge. Upon arrival, the cadets fell in march along with the Confederate army of 4,500 men and soon found Sigel's 6,500 Federal troops entrenched near the town of New Market, Virginia. Breckinridge engaged the enemy on May 15, first trying to spare the 247 V.M.I. teenagers. When the Union troops counterattacked, and threatened to destroy the Confederate center, Breckinridge reluctantly ordered the cadets to enter the fray. Engaging in dramatic hand-to-hand combat, the cadets and Rebel regulars overran the Federals and forced them from the field. In the struggle, ten cadets lost their lives, and another forty-seven received wounds. Their victory at New Market, however, would forever become a symbol of youthful heroism.[20]

Student cadets seldom achieved such success on the battlefield. The cadet corps from Virginia's Roanoke College in Salem would have an equally harrowing tale of their military adventures before the war was over, but without the tenor of victory shared by their V.M.I. counterparts. On the morning of December 16, 1863, four regiments of Federal mounted infantry, a cavalry battalion, and an artillery battery swarmed into the college town. Although the boys had trained for two years, the Union raid caught them completely by surprise. As some of the Federal troops burned the army supplies stored in the town, others rounded up citizens and students and placed them under guard. After a night of being held prisoner, the students were brought before the commanding Union general, William W. Averell, who questioned each student, asking where he came from. The young men held fast with closed-mouthed defiance, prompting the general to say, "Come now boys, tell me candidly what you think of the Confederacy." This statement elicited a prompt, patriotic response from the students. "We think its doing very well," they answered. "O now, boys, you know it is most played out," the general continued, adding, "you all go back to your books and study your best." Averell then ordered that they be released to return to their studies.[21]

Proceeding with studies as normal was a tall order for students in southern colleges during the war. They craved news of the fighting and felt isolated, driving their concentration to distraction. Georgian Gratz Cohen illustrated the problems with trying to remain simply a student in wartime when he wrote to his father from the University of Virginia in the summer of 1862, "I look impatiently to my newspaper, for here we are out of the world, hearing only the faintest rumor of a rumor, like one, who, at a great distance, sees a cloud of dust, but not able to tell whether tis made by friend or foe—men or cattle." His studies were also affected by the events of the times. He still wanted his parents to lower their expectations of his academic success, but he also did not want to leave the relative safety of the classroom for the battlefield. In another letter to his parents, he began by writing that there was an "utter impossibility of giving an undivided attention to my studies at times like these" and that this situation had "rendered complete success impossible." He also told them that several students were considering leaving the university because they thought their attempts at learning were in vain. Cohen disagreed, stating that "though complete attention to studies is impossible, I still feel that I can do more here than any where else and that tho'

I may not have learned as much as I would have, at another time, still I know infinitely more of German, Latin, History & Literature than I did last year."[22]

Before Cohen's college career was over, that "cloud of dust" would come closer to him, creating even more difficulties for his studies. In May of 1863 Cohen wrote to his father that he was taking his final examinations. Early in the letter he explained that he had already finished his history examination, "tho' the result has not yet been made known." He further asserted that his examinations in French and German were to take place within the next week. Then Cohen's narrative took a harrowing turn. He reported that on a Sunday, when most of the students were at church, he was nearly alone at the university. A student arrived with information that Federal cavalry was approaching Charlottesville and that Gen. Robert E. Lee had appealed for volunteers to cut them off. Young Cohen then went into great detail describing the next few days, in which the students formed a company and camped near Monticello waiting for the Yankee raid. After several days the threat had subsided and the students had gone back to the university. He wrote: "I was tired out but the examination for German was to be on Thursday & I had but two days to prepare for it so I had to study. To day the examination took place. I have no idea that I passed through it. My mind is completely unhinged, indeed every one at the University is in the same condition." The last point of the letter, however, was for Cohen to inform his father that he did not expect to pass the French examination. He asserted, "I hate to write this, & you I know will feel pained to hear it but my only consolation is that at another time I could & would have [done] better, but this year it seems that as soon as I would get studying some thing would happen to interrupt me."[23] Perhaps more than any other student writing home to explain poor performance at college, Cohen had found the perfect excuse—Yankees.

Many students found themselves in situations similar to Cohen's, with the war encroaching upon their collegiate lives. University of Virginia student Launcelot Blackford wrote to his mother that the campus had become the site of a military hospital. There were so many wounded men in the area in July 1861 that the Confederate hospital in Charlottesville could not serve them all. As a result, the university served as an overflow hospital, where "along in the Public Hall, Chapel, and on the Lawns," there were nearly three hundred wounded men being treated. Because of a shortage of physicians and nurses, most of the students took turns attending to the wounded. Blackford wrote of this experience: "I have become accustomed to seeing the fearful sights, mutilations, etc. already, but some of the worst cases I cannot—nor ever can I believe—look upon with anything like professional stolidity."[24]

Having the war so close to the University of Virginia, and other universities in the South, also meant that students could occasionally visit friends who had already enlisted. Cornelius Dabney, the younger brother of Robert Dabney, who had attended Hampden-Sidney and the University of Virginia in the decade before, enjoyed just such an opportunity. Cornelius recounted that the 2nd Virginia Cavalry was camped near Charlottesville in the winter of 1863. One of his friends learned that Robert Dabney was in the camp, located three miles from the town. "This evening, he and I walked out there, and found him after much difficulty," reported Cornelius. It is clear that Cornelius would have had a difficult time if he were in the army. He wrote of this visit that he was "so fatigued by my walk that I did not go to church tonight."[25]

Although the war was ever-present, nevertheless, the privileged adolescents who remained in school settled into a reasonable facsimile of college life. Their daily routines little resembled those of their comrades on the battlefield. In describing his life at the University of Virginia in 1862, Gratz Cohen told his parents: "At six we take our supper. Then I generally linger in one of the students' rooms till seven & then retire to my own to study & by ten, having finished, I am almost always in bed and asleep. The next morning about 3/6 [5:45 A.M.] a heavy knock, if I am not already awake, rouses me from my slumbers, it is Davis [presumably a slave], who comes to bring water and clean my boots. I get up & dress myself and then go to breakfast."

The son of a wealthy Georgia planter, Cohen took his meals at a local Charlottesville boardinghouse. In October 1862 he described to his family the "bill of fare" for one of his meals: "Soup, Fillet of veal stuffed, Roast chickens, Ham, cold beef & mutton, vegetables, Irish & Sweet potatoes, corn, stewed tomatoes, Salad, Tomatoes, Dessert, Stewed apples, & milk." He also enjoyed special gifts of food from his family.

"I received the box safely from the hands of Cyrus and cannot tell you what a treat it was," he wrote to his parents. "I actually lived last week on its contents and while it lasted would every night invite some of the boys to have supper with me. . . . I really believe that I do not eat as much during the week here as I did at home in one day. I can give you no idea how miserably wretched the food is. When Frank comes up if you can get any kind of pickles—cucumbers (salt & water) or biscuits they will be most acceptable."[26]

For many college students, life continued much like Cohen's. They concerned themselves with the same endeavors that had driven all previous generations of southern college boys. They struggled with their studies, taunted their professors, courted young women, and behaved as adolescents concerned with their place in the world. Student-cadet Reuben Boling of the University of Alabama played his role thoroughly, as seen in a letter to his mother in the winter of 1864. In this communication, he expressed little concern about the war or any other event of the times. He was most interested in his clothes. He had asked his mother to send some cloth so the university tailor could make him another uniform. He reported that cloth would not be available to the university for several months, and he wanted her to send enough to make one suit. He told her: "I want you to cut the pants at home, in the stile of my last not quite so large, as I do not like the stile up here and the old Tailor wont cut any other stile." He added, "I had rather have my jacket cut up here, as they cut a very pretty jacket."[27] In a world still dictated by honor, appearance was everything.

College boys also continued their social lives during the war. Drinking, dancing, courting, and other forms of social enjoyment remained constant on the southern campuses that remained open during the war. Cornelius Dabney, a devout Baptist at the University of Virginia, reported some of these social events in 1863. Although his personal taste was more toward prayer meetings, on November 19 he penned in his diary that "a grand soiree given by the students occurred last night. There were no refreshments, and the chief, and for aught I know, only amusement was dancing." He added piously, "I of course did not attend." Dabney did, however, join in the pursuit of female companionship—although without much success. In October 1863 he made the following entry in his diary: "In the evening Luther and I according to a previous engagement between ourselves fixed up & sullied forth to call on Miss Nannie Abell but did not find her at home." The two young Lotharios were determined, so they "bought a pack of visiting cards, and walked to Mr. Fife's intending to ask two of the young ladies to walk to church with us." When they arrived, a young lady—Miss Kate Fife— escorted them into the parlor, where they were surprised to find the object of their original affections, Nannie Abell. She quickly departed, leaving the two in the parlor. Undaunted, Dabney reported that they "found that the [Fife] ladies had already determined to go to church. We therefore tactily offered our arms to the ladies with whom we had intended to walk. When church was over, however, they asserted, that we had not called on them with the intention of going to church, and therefore they would not consent to our walking so far to escort them home. We protested, but they remained inexorable and we were compelled to submit to our fate."[28]

Despite these vestiges of normal college life on campuses throughout the South, the hardships of war would eventually alter them all. One of the greatest difficulties was to feed students at a time when fields were left untended and every available morsel was finding its way to the troops. One Hampden-Sidney student remembered that at the boardinghouse where he lived "rations were scarce," but the owner "gave us sufficient to 'stay our stummicks' as Uncle Remus would say." He elaborated: "The coffee was rye parched and sweetened with sorghum. Wheat bread was unknown and our daily diet was corn bread, bacon and black-eyed peas." For boys who were used to having wider variety and quantities at their meals, such daily fare was not enough. "This diet," he concluded, "was frequently reinforced by rabbits caught by the boys in snares."[29]

As the war continued, however, food became even more scarce. In April 1865, Hampden-Sidney students found themselves directly in the path of Gen. Robert E. Lee's retreat from Petersburg to Appomattox. Days before the Army of Northern Virginia surrendered, there was no food left at the college. In a search for something to eat, the students made their way to Farmville, just seven miles away. One student described the scene, asserting that as they entered the town, they "found everything in confusion. Many wounded were arriving and, as usual, the ladies were busy aiding them in every way they could, giving them food and the best of the little they had left." In their state of hunger, the students eyed the handouts with great desire. One student later regretted his actions of that day. He wrote: "I blush with shame to confess an act of at least indirect deception, perpetrated by myself. I had at the time a bad boil over my eye with a bandage on it, which was mistaken by the ladies for a bullet hole. I was approached by several of them and given both much sympathy and 'eats.' The latter was the more acceptable as I was good and hungry."[30]

College and university presidents found it difficult to balance the need to maintain a large enough enrollment to stay open with the difficult task of feeding those in their institutions. Roanoke College president Daniel Bittle worked hard at this balancing act, using revolutionary and creative ideas to feed the students and keep the school open. During the course of the war, Roanoke students spent time making ersatz food in addition to attending to their studies. They made molasses from sorghum and drank coffee made of parched rye, sweetened with their molasses.

These substitutions, however, met only part of the wartime challenge. Enrollment woes threatened to close the college because of dwindling tuition. To meet this threat, President Bittle announced a stunning change in admission policies: Roanoke College began admitting women. Although they were to attend classes separate from the males, women students provided enough tuition to counter the effect of losing so many young men to the army. Ultimately, Roanoke's location in Salem (in western Virginia) and its relative isolation from the war saved it. Virginia parents who lived in the path of the fighting began to send their sons to Roanoke because it offered them a measure of safety. After only two sessions, Bittle discontinued the admission of women, as the male enrollments had increased enough to pay the bills.

During the two sessions with a coeducational system, however, college life at Roanoke was far from "normal" for the era. The presence of young ladies changed social activities of the school. During one of the sessions they attended, both male and female students staged a series of grand tableaux to raise funds for Confederate hospitals. These popular dramatic forms in which the participants posed themselves in costumes to depict a famous historical event or painting proved to be quite successful. President Bittle wrote in 1875 of these performances that they "proved to be one of the most magnificent exhibitions that Salem ever saw. They realized over thirteen hundred dollars from one evening's performance." He praised the students for bringing Roanoke College to one of "her proudest occasions." The students performed "The Mock Court," "The Marriage of Pocahontas," "The Songs of the Muses," and "scenes from sacred history," all performed "in such a way as they never saw it done before or since."[31]

Other universities faced the challenges of enrollment and food shortages in different manners. For the University of Alabama, its reputation as a military training school kept its numbers high. President Landon Garland recognized that in a time of war, military preparation took precedence over academics, and he advertised this all over the state. The marketing effort worked, gaining the support of the state legislature to keep the university open. Garland insisted that the cadets continue their academic study in between sessions of close-order drill. Whereas the university's enrollment had been eighty-one students in 1860–1861, by the middle of the war Garland had to order tents to house the ballooning number of students coming to his institution from all over Alabama, Mississippi, and Georgia. By 1863, there were more than 260 cadets enrolled at the university. Garland even came up with an ingenious plan to handle feeding so many—in 1863 the university passed a requirement that every cadet enrolled in the institution would have to bring two hundred pounds of bacon with him before he would be admitted.[32]

Of course, in the end, none of these measures would stem the tide of the losing war being fought by the sons of the South. Southern colleges and universities would eventually have to submit, along with the rest of society, to the stronger armies of the United States. The end was harsh for those institutions that had remained open during the war. The fates of Washington College, the Virginia Military Institute, and the University of Alabama were representative of the end for the southern collegiate system.

On Sunday morning, June 12, 1864, Union major general David Hunter led his Army of Western Virginia on a raid into the town of

Lexington. Union troops sacked the town, but paid special destructive attention to the buildings of Washington College and the Virginia Military Institute. With both colleges being owned and operated by the state, Union troops prepared to burn them to the ground. In retribution for the activities of V.M.I.'s cadets at New Market, and in recognition that Confederate major general Thomas J. "Stonewall" Jackson had served as professor of natural and experimental philosophy there, Hunter's soldiers sent V.M.I.'s buildings into a blazing conflagration by midday. When Washington College's trustees arrived, however, they pleaded that their institution was strictly a civil organization and that George Washington had provided the funds to start it. These arguments saved its buildings from destruction. Nevertheless, Federal troops destroyed all scientific apparatus and burned books and papers from both institutions, resulting in the need for the schools to be restored before another class would ever again be held at either.[33]

Similarly, the spring of 1865 would bring destruction to Alabama's premier university. Union major general J. H. Wilson moved into the state at that time and ordered one of his brigades, under the command of Gen. John Croxton, to destroy the town of Tuscaloosa adjacent to the university. At 12:30 on the morning of April 4, the cadets were roused from sleep with the alarm that the Federals were in the town. They quickly formed into their companies and detached a squad to retrieve their artillery from a livery stable where it had been hidden. The cadets double-quick marched in column down the road toward the town center and formed in a line of battle on a hill overlooking the town. Their tightly drawn battle plan fell apart, however, when they learned that the Federals had already captured their artillery and the squad that had been sent to retrieve it. By 1:00 A.M. the town had officially surrendered, and the cadets had to retreat back to the university without firing a shot.

Dr. Garland decided that the cadets should not be captured, so he ordered them to retreat from the university. As they marched away, the students heard the explosion from the detonation of the campus ammunition depot. They saw the flames rising from the university as Croxton's brigade destroyed almost every building on the campus. On April 5, Garland furloughed the cadets, ordering them to reassemble on May 12 at a place to be designated. But they never did come back together, as news of Lee's, Johnston's, and Taylor's surrenders arrived before May 12. The war was over.[34]

For the boys of the South who had experienced college life before this point in history, the end of the Civil War marked the death knell for an era. The sons of the southern gentry had lived in a time in which the code of honor was the driving spirit that guided their adolescent path to adulthood. This code has been described by numerous modern scholars, who have defined it as "that constellation of ideas and values in which one's sense of self-worth rested on the degree of respect commanded from others in the community."[35] They have shown us that southern honor consisted of a set of rules that advanced the *appearance* of duty, pride, power, and self-esteem, and conformity to these rules was required if an individual were to be considered an honorable member of society. Within this system defined by honor, "one's existence and even one's capacity or right to survive are determined in the public forum."[36] And they have further shown that "honor and dishonor, like mastery and slavery, were total conditions."[37]

The Civil War, therefore, represented the ultimate test of the code of honor for the South. To preserve the system of plantation slavery from which the southern college boys had emerged, the South represented itself—its "public face"—as a nation capable of separating from the Union. When Lincoln called for seventy-five thousand volunteers to put down the rebellion, southerners responded to the "challenge"; they were willing to defend their "nation" with their lives. In this duel of nations, college students responded to the call to support this public decision. Colleges and universities closed all over the South as young men left their books behind to protect honor by taking up arms in defense of their southern identity. And at institutions that continued to function during the war, students tried to persevere through hardships to continue to define themselves as southern college men, just as those who had passed before them had done. In the South's attempt to defend its identity as a nation, however, it failed. But according to the code to which southerners adhered, honor had been defended. Even though the Confederacy fell, it had met an honorable end. Nevertheless, the college life of the Old South died with it.

It is clear that antebellum southern college students had created their own culture within the larger context of southern honor. Their reactions to curriculum and faculty, their sense of pride in their institutions, their interactions with their college environment and classmates, their search for amusements and relationships, and their tendency toward violence all stemmed from their creation of a peer-defined code of honor linked to the culture of the South. When the dominant southern culture came tumbling down at the hands of Federal troops, college life in the South fell with it.

After the Civil War, southern colleges and universities rebuilt and began again, but changes in the society dictated new constructs for the lives of students. Literary societies, the basic social and intellectual organizations on southern campuses, eventually gave way to more strictly social fraternities. Close adherence to gender roles in southern colleges eventually gave way to coeducational institutions of higher learning. And the changing class structure of the South would eventually open college doors to a wider variety of students. None of these changes occurred overnight. And of course adolescence would continue to be a driving force for defining college student behavior from that time to this. However, it was the Civil War's transformation of the role of honor—the South's self-concept—that would be the catalyst for changing how southern college students tread the path to adulthood. College life in the South would never be the same again.

Notes

ABBREVIATIONS

ADAH   Alabama Department of Archives and History, Montgomery, Alabama.

AU   Special Collections, Auburn University Library, Auburn, Alabama.

DU   Special Collections Library, Duke University, Durham, North Carolina.

GHS   Georgia Historical Society, Savannah, Georgia.

SHC   Southern Historical Collection, University of North Carolina, Chapel Hill.

UA   Hoole Library Special Collections, University of Alabama, Tuscaloosa.

UVA-Alderman   Alderman Library Special Collections, University of Virginia, Charlottesville.

UVA-Wilson   Wilson Library, University of Virginia, Charlottesville, Virginia.

VMI   Virginia Military Institute Archives, Virginia Military Institute, Lexington.

INTRODUCTION

1. See the Andrew McCollam Papers, SHC.

2. E. Merton Coulter, *College Life in the Old South: As Seen at the University of Georgia* (New York: Macmillan, 1928; reprint, Athens: Univ. of Georgia Press, 1983), xv–xvi.

3. Helen Lefkowitz Horowitz, *Campus Life: Undergraduate Cultures from the End of the Eighteenth Century to the Present* (Chapel Hill: Univ. of North Carolina Press, 1995), ix–x.

4. Ibid., 23, 27–9.

5. Ibid., 81.

6. Ibid., 31–4.

7. Bertram Wyatt-Brown's definition of southern honor in *Southern Honor: Ethics and Behavior in the Old South* (New York and Oxford: Oxford Univ. Press, 1982), xv. On honor and southern society, see Peter W. Bardaglio, *Reconstructing the Household: Families, Sex,*

and the Law in the Nineteenth-Century South, Studies in Legal History, edited by Thomas A. Green and Hendrik Hartog (Chapel Hill: Univ. of North Carolina Press, 1995), 22–3.

8. On cognitive change during adolescence, see Jean Piaget, *Six Psychological Studies* (New York: Random House, 1968), 61; Henry Markovitz et al., "Reasoning in Young Children: Fantasy and Information-Retrieval," *Child Development* 67 (1996): 2857–72; and Deanna Kuhn et al., "The Development of Formal Operations in Logical and Moral Judgment," *Genetic Psychology Monographs* 95 (1977): 97–188.

9. L. Ray Drinkwater, "Honor and Student Misconduct in Southern Antebellum Colleges," *Southern Humanities Review* 27 (fall 1993): 329.

10. Samuel Eliot Morison, *Three Centuries of Harvard, 1636–1836* (Cambridge, Mass.: Harvard Univ. Press, 1936), 199. For further discussion of the differences between southern honor and northern gentility, see Kenneth S. Greenberg, *Honor and Slavery: Lies, Duels, Noses, Masks, Dressing as a Woman, Gifts, Strangers, Humanitarianism, Death, Slave Rebellions, the Proslavery Argument, Baseball, Hunting, and Gambling in the Old South* (Princeton, N.J.: Princeton Univ. Press, 1996), 11; and Wyatt-Brown, *Southern Honor,* 96–7.

11. Wyatt-Brown, *Southern Honor,* xii.

12. Bardaglio, *Reconstructing the Household,* 5.

13. Greenberg, *Honor and Slavery,* 62; for a discussion of modern regional differences related to the code of honor, see Dov Cohen, Joseph Vandello, and Adrian K. Rantilla, "The Sacred and the Social: Honor and Violence in Cultural Context," in *Shame: Interpersonal Behavior, Psychopathology, and Culture,* edited by Paul Gilbert and Bernice Andrews, Series in Affective Science (Cambridge: Oxford Univ. Press, 1998), 261–82.

14. See Edith H. Altbach, "Vanguard of Revolt: Students and Politics in Central Europe, 1815–1848," in *Students in Revolt,* edited by Seymour Martin Lipset and Philip G. Altbach (Boston: Houghton Mifflin, 1969), 451–74; Konrad H. Jarausch, "The Sources of German Student Unrest, 1815–1848," in *The University in Society: Volume II, Europe, Scotland, and the United States from the 16th to the 20th Century,* edited by Lawrence Stone (Princeton, N.J.: Princeton Univ. Press, 1974), 533–69.

15. Christie Anne Farnham, *The Education of the Southern Belle: Higher Education and Student Socialization in the Antebellum South* (New York and London: New York Univ. Press, 1994), 121.

16. For a full treatment of higher education and southern women, see ibid. For broader treatments of women's roles in southern society and culture, see Elizabeth Fox-Genovese, *Within the Plantation Household: Black and White Women in the Old South* (Chapel Hill: Univ. of North Carolina Press, 1988); and Catherine Clinton, *The Plantation Mistress: Woman's World in the Old South* (New York: Pantheon, 1982).

1. IT'S ALL ACADEMIC

1. "Alvarus Pelagius on the Faults of Scholars," in *University Records and Life in the Middle Ages,* edited by Lynn Thorndyke (New York: Columbia Univ. Press, 1944; reprint, New York: W. W. Norton, 1975), 173.

2. B. C. Lee to Mother, November 11, 1859, B. C. Lee Letter, AU.

3. George Little to John Little, November 26, 1859, and January 13, 1860, Little Family Papers, UA.

4. L. Ray Drinkwater, "Honor and Student Misconduct in Southern Antebellum Colleges," *Southern Humanities Review* 27 (fall 1993): 338 n. 88.

5. Quoted in William Edward Eisenberg, *The First Hundred Years, Roanoke College, 1842–1942* (Salem, Va.: Trustees of Roanoke College, 1942), 38–9.

6. James Lee Jr. to G. A. Henry, October 20, 1850, Gustavus A. Henry Papers, SHC.

7. J. F. Henry to Mrs. G. A. Henry, October 4, 1856, Gustavus A. Henry Papers, SHC.

8. Chas. Minor Blackford to Launcelot M. Blackford, March 4, 1852, B. Lewis Blackford Letters, SHC.

9. Robert Philip Howell Memoirs, SHC, 1.

10. Robert E. Cutler to Robert C. Cutler, September 15, 1834, Joel Leftwich Papers, UVA-Alderman.

11. R. L. Dabney to Elizabeth Dabney, June 23, 1836, Papers of the Dabney Family, UVA-Alderman. Although named for English patriots John Hampden and Algernon Sydney at its founding in 1776, Hampden-Sydney College was most often spelled "Hampden-Sidney" in the nineteenth century. I will use this spelling convention throughout this book.

12. E. Merton Coulter, *College Life in the Old South: As Seen at the University of Georgia* (New York: Macmillan, 1928; reprint, Athens: Univ. of Georgia Press, 1983), 66.

13. For a full discussion of the relationship between class status and threats to honor, see Kenneth S. Greenberg, *Honor and Slavery: Lies, Duels, Noses, Masks, Dressing as a Woman, Gifts, Strangers, Humanitarianism, Death, Slave Rebellions, the Proslavery Argument, Baseball, Hunting, and Gambling in the Old South* (Princeton, N.J.: Princeton Univ. Press, 1996).

14. James Mercer Garnett Jr. to Mary E. Garnett, November 23, 1811, Papers of the Hunter-Garnett Families, UVA-Alderman.

15. J. D. Tatum to Anna Tatum, September 30, 1856, John Dudley Tatum Letters, SHC.

16. Edward C. Anderson Jr. to Father, January 1, 1858, Wayne-Stites-Anderson Papers, GHS.

17. R. L. Dabney to Charles W. Dabney, December 15, 1841, Papers of the Dabney Family, UVA-Alderman.

18. James I. Robertson Jr., *Stonewall Jackson: The Man, the Soldier, the Legend* (New York: Macmillan, 1997), 122.

19. R. L. Dabney to Charles W. Dabney, July 5, 1837, Papers of the Dabney Family, UVA-Alderman.

20. Lowrie J. Daly, *The Medieval University, 1200–1400* (New York: Sheed and Ward, 1961), 8.

21. Helen Lefkowitz Horowitz, *Campus Life: Undergraduate Cultures from the End of*

the Eighteenth Century to the Present (Chapel Hill: Univ. of North Carolina Press, 1995), 26. For a full discussion of the evolution of American curriculum in the nineteenth century, see Frederick Rudolph, *Curriculum: A History of the American Undergraduate Course of Study since 1636* (San Francisco: Jossey-Bass, 1977), 54–98.

22. Rudolph, *Curriculum,* 57. Bertram Wyatt-Brown agrees with this thesis, contending that southern whites held on to the classical Greek and Latin literature as the basis of southern colleges because it reassured them that "nothing much need change; the past was yet alive." He further argues that "the South's concern with classical sources reflected the continued relevance of Stoic traditions of honor and virtue." Wyatt-Brown, *Southern Honor,* 93, 95.

23. D. Wyatt Aiken Autobiography [typescript], SHC, 5–6.

24. James Edward Scanlon, *Randolph-Macon College: A Southern History, 1825–1967* (Charlottesville: Univ. Press of Virginia, 1983), 72.

25. Ibid., 73.

26. R. L. Dabney to Charles W. Dabney, September 8, 1834, Papers of the Dabney Family, UVA-Alderman.

27. William Sydney Mullins Diary, October 26, 1840, SHC.

28. R. L. Dabney to Elizabeth Dabney, September 24, 1834, Papers of the Dabney Family, UVA-Alderman.

29. Thomas R. Martin to Ma, October 13, 1860, John S. Martin Papers, SHC.

30. William Sydney Mullins Diary, July 26, 1840, SHC.

31. James Lee Jr. to G. A. Henry, October 20, 1850, Gustavus A. Henry Papers, SHC.

32. James Gwyn Diary, November 22, 1850, SHC.

33. R. L. Dabney to Elizabeth Dabney, June 3, 1837, and November 6, 1836, Papers of the Dabney Family, UVA-Alderman.

34. Quoted in Lisa Tolbert, ed., *Two Hundred Years of Student Life at Chapel Hill: Selected Letters and Diaries* (Chapel Hill, N.C.: Center for the Study of the American South, IRSS Faculty Working Group in Southern Studies, 1993), 24.

35. William Sydney Mullins Diary, November 12, 1840, SHC.

36. R. L. Dabney to Mary Dabney, July 23, 1836, Papers of the Dabney Family, UVA-Alderman.

37. Hector Jas. McNeill to Father and Mother, August 18, 1854, Hector James McNeill Letters, SHC.

38. James Mercer Garnett Jr. to Mary E. Garnett, November 23, 1811, Papers of the Hunter-Garnett Families, UVA-Alderman.

39. John F. Henry to Tadry Henry, November 1, 1856, Gustavus A. Henry Papers, SHC.

40. Tolbert, ed., *Two Hundred Years,* 50.

41. William Sydney Mullins Diary, March 1, 1841, SHC.

42. Quoted in Tolbert, ed., *Two Hundred Years,* 50.

43. James Mercer Garnett Jr. to Mary E. Garnett, November 23, 1811, Papers of the Hunter-Garnett Families, UVA-Alderman.

44. James Allen Cabaniss, *The University of Mississippi: Its First Hundred Years,* 2nd ed. (Hattiesburg: Univ. College Press of Mississippi, 1971), 49.

45. Diary of Basil Manly II (no. 4, 1848–1857), p. 5–6, Manly Family Papers, UA.

46. Coulter, *College Life in the Old South,* 134–48.

47. Quoted in Carolyn L. Blair and Arda S. Walker, *By Faith Endowed: The Story of Maryville College, 1819–1994* (Maryville, Tenn.: Maryville College Press, 1994), 21.

48. William H. Burwell to Father, April 23, 1855, Boyd Family Papers, SHC.

49. William Blackledge Whitfield Diary, April 12, 1860, William Blackledge Whitfield Papers, SHC.

50. R. L. Dabney to Charles W. Dabney, March 16, 1837, Papers of the Dabney Family, UVA-Alderman.

51. William Hamilton Nelson, *A Burning Torch and a Flaming Fire: The Story of Centenary College of Louisiana* (Nashville, Tenn.: Methodist Publishing House, 1931), 140–2.

52. William Blackledge Whitfield Diary, May 3, 1860, William Blackledge Whitfield Papers, SHC.

53. Quoted in Scanlon, *Randolph-Macon College,* 75–6.

2. ON CAMPUS

1. William Edward Eisenberg, *The First Hundred Years, Roanoke College, 1842–1942* (Salem, Va.: Trustees of Roanoke College, 1942), 38–9.

2. T. R. Caldwell to John Caldwell, August 2, 1837, John Caldwell Papers, SHC.

3. Lisa Tolbert, ed., *Two Hundred Years of Student Life at Chapel Hill: Selected Letters and Diaries* (Chapel Hill, N.C.: Center for the Study of the American South, IRSS Faculty Working Group in Southern Studies, 1993), 28; William H. Burwell to Mother, January 16, 1853, Boyd Family Papers, SHC.

4. George Penn to Eliza Penn, January 5, 1842, Elizabeth Seawell Penn Hairston Papers, SHC.

5. Willoughby Tebbs to W. Leroy Broun, October 2, 1846, William Leroy Broun Papers, AU.

6. Robert Whitehead to Floyd L. Whitehead, October 1, 1830, Papers of Floyd L. Whitehead, UVA-Alderman.

7. Leonidas F. Siler to Sarah A. Jarrett, September 8, 1846, Sarah A. Jarrett Papers, SHC.

8. William H. Burwell to Father, August 22, 1852, Boyd Family Papers, SHC.

9. F. M. Johnson to Jinnie Johnson, August 20, 1857, Nathan Wilson Walker Papers, SHC.

10. J. F. Henry to Mrs. G. A. Henry, October 4, 1856, Gustavus A. Henry Papers, SHC.

11. William Gibson Field Journal [typescript], p. 11, UVA-Wilson.

12. Edward C. Anderson Jr. to Mother, October 25, 1857, Wayne-Stites-Anderson Papers, GHS.

13. Edward C. Anderson Jr. to Father, October 1, 1858, ibid.

14. James Mercer Garnett Jr. to James Mercer Garnett Sr., November 20, 1811, Papers of the Hunter-Garnett Families, UVA-Alderman.

15. N. F. Neal to Father and Mother, September 2, 1857, Neal Family Papers, SHC.

16. Poem on fleas, 1858, George Knox Miller Papers, SHC.

17. Ollinger Crenshaw, *General Lee's College: The Rise and Growth of Washington and Lee University* (New York: Random House, 1969), 97.

18. T. R. Caldwell to Father, February 25, 1837, John Caldwell Papers, SHC.

19. Quoted in John Luster Brinkley, *On This Hill: A Narrative History of Hampden-Sydney College, 1774–1994* (Hampden-Sydney, Va.: [Hampden-Sydney College], 1994), 206.

20. Tolbert, ed., *Two Hundred Years,* 27–8.

21. R. L. Dabney to Elizabeth Dabney, November 9, 1836, Papers of the Dabney Family, UVA-Alderman.

22. William Blackledge Whitfield Diary, May 2, 1860, William Blackledge Whitfield Papers, SHC.

23. George Penn to Eliza Penn, January 5, 1842, Elizabeth Seawell Penn Hairston Papers, SHC.

24. William Hamilton Nelson, *A Burning Torch and a Flaming Fire: The Story of Centenary College of Louisiana* (Nashville, Tenn.: Methodist Publishing House, 1931), 170–1.

25. Edward C. Anderson Jr. to Mother, November 8, 1857, Wayne-Stites-Anderson Papers, GHS.

26. Thomas R. Martin to Brother, October 13, 1860, and Thomas R. Martin to Ma, November 16, 1860, John S. Martin Papers, SHC.

27. Robert Whitehead to Floyd L. Whitehead, July 1, 1833, Papers of Floyd L. Whitehead, UVA-Alderman.

28. Edward C. Anderson Jr. to Mother, November 12, 1857, Wayne-Stites-Anderson Papers, GHS.

29. Leroy Broun to Sallie Fleming, January 4, 1849, William Leroy Broun Papers, AU.

30. Edward C. Anderson Jr. to Father, January 1, 1858, and Edward C. Anderson Jr. to Mother, January 6, 1858, Wayne-Stites-Anderson Papers, GHS.

31. G. K. Miller to Cellie McCann, December 13, 1860, George Knox Miller Papers, SHC.

32. John D. Wright Jr., *Transylvania: Tutor to the West* (Lexington, Ky.: Univ. Press of Kentucky, 1975), 93.

33. Andrew McCollam Jr. to Father, October 10, 1860, Andrew McCollam Papers, SHC.

34. R. L. Dabney to Charles W. Dabney, March 16, 1837, Papers of the Dabney Family, UVA-Alderman.

35. Tolbert, ed., *Two Hundred Years,* 30–1.

36. William Sydney Mullins Diary, February 20, 1841, SHC.

37. James Gwyn Diary, October 8–9, 1850, SHC.

38. Edward C. Anderson Jr. to Mother, December 30, 1857, Wayne-Stites-Anderson Papers, GHS.

39. William Blackledge Whitfield Diary, April 14, 1860, William Blackledge Whitfield Papers, SHC.

40. Edward C. Anderson Jr. to Father, June 1, 1857, and Edward C. Anderson Jr. to Mother, December 9 and 30, 1857, Wayne-Stites-Anderson Papers, GHS.

41. J. F. Henry to Pat Henry, February 22, 1857, Gustavus A. Henry Papers, SHC.

42. Quoted in Wright, *Transylvania*, 125.

43. William Gibson Field Journal [typescript], p. 18, UVA-Alderman.

44. Virginius Dabney, *Mr. Jefferson's University: A History* (Charlottesville: Univ. Press of Virginia, 1981), 19.

45. James Gwyn Diary, October 15, 1850, SHC.

46. Diary of Basil Manly II (no. 3, 1843–1848), January 19 and 25, 1844, Manly Family Papers, UA.

47. Ibid., March 4, 1846.

48. For a full discussion of the role of honor in the southern slave society, see Kenneth S. Greenberg, *Honor and Slavery: Lies, Duels, Noses, Masks, Dressing as a Woman, Gifts, Strangers, Humanitarianism, Death, Slave Rebellions, the Proslavery Argument, Baseball, Hunting, and Gambling in the Old South* (Princeton, N.J.: Princeton Univ. Press, 1996).

49. James Allen Cabaniss, *The University of Mississippi: Its First Hundred Years,* 2nd ed. (Hattiesburg: Univ. College Press of Mississippi, 1971), 46–8.

50. Robert E. Cutler to Robert C. Cutler, December 14, 1833, Joel Leftwich Papers, UVA-Alderman.

51. Quoted in Wright, *Transylvania*, 94.

52. William Gibson Field Journal [typescript], pp. 6–7, UVA-Wilson.

53. R. L. Dabney to Elizabeth Dabney, May 8, 1840, Papers of the Dabney Family, UVA-Alderman.

54. R. L. Dabney to Charles W. Dabney, September 8, 1834, ibid.

55. Robert Whitehead to Floyd L. Whitehead, February 15, 1831, Papers of Floyd L. Whitehead, UVA-Alderman.

56. R. L. Dabney to Elizabeth Dabney, November 9, 1836, Papers of the Dabney Family, UVA-Alderman.

57. John Jones to Thomas Jones, September 8, 1811, Thomas Williamson Jones Letters, SHC.

58. Edward C. Anderson Jr. to Mother, February 19, 1858, Wayne-Stites-Anderson Papers, GHS.

3. SOWING OATS AND GROWING UP

1. H. J. McNeill to Father, October 27, 1854, Hector James McNeill Letters, SHC.

2. Hector Jas. McNeill to Father and Mother, August 18, 1854, ibid.

3. David M. Lees to Hugh M. Lees, March 17, 1824, David McMichen Lees Papers, SHC.

4. Henry R. Bryan to Ma, May 12, 1855, Mary Biddle Norcott Bryan Scrapbook, SHC.

5. R. L. Dabney to Charles W. Dabney, July 5, 1836, Papers of the Dabney Family, UVA-Alderman.

6. Diary of Basil Manly II (no. 4, 1848–1857), July 4, 1849, Manly Family Papers, UA.

7. Robert Whitehead to Floyd L. Whitehead, February 15, 1831, Papers of Floyd L. Whitehead, UVA-Alderman.

8. William Sydney Mullins Diary, January 21, 1841, SHC.

9. William Blackledge Whitfield Diary, April 14, 1860, William Blackledge Whitfield Papers, SHC.

10. A. M. McCollam Jr. to Mother, February 1, 1860, Andrew McCollam Papers, SHC.

11. William Gibson Field Journal [typescript], p. 22, UVA-Wilson.

12. Light Townsend Cummins, *Austin College: A Sesquicentennial History, 1849–1999* (Austin: Eakin Press, 1999), 45–6.

13. John F. Henry to Tadry Henry, November 1, 1856, Gustavus A. Henry Papers, SHC.

14. R. L. Dabney to Elizabeth Dabney, March 19, 1837, Papers of the Dabney Family, UVA-Alderman.

15. Quoted in Lisa Tolbert, ed., *Two Hundred Years of Student Life at Chapel Hill: Selected Letters and Diaries* (Chapel Hill, N.C.: Center for the Study of the American South, IRSS Faculty Working Group in Southern Studies, 1993), 65–6.

16. Quoted ibid., 69.

17. William Blackledge Whitfield Diary, April 29 and May 2, 1860, William Blackledge Whitfield Papers, SHC.

18. Thomas R. Martin to Brother, January 30, 1860 [1861], John S. Martin Papers, SHC.

19. Virginius Dabney, *Mr. Jefferson's University: A History* (Charlottesville: Univ. Press of Virginia, 1981), 12, 20.

20. William Sydney Mullins Diary, February 5, 1841, SHC.

21. Leroy Broun to Sallie Fleming, January 4, 1849, William Leroy Broun Papers, AU.

22. Edward C. Anderson Jr. to Mother, December 9, 1857, and January 6 and 27, 1858, Wayne-Stites-Anderson Papers, GHS.

23. William Sydney Mullins Diary, October 26 and November 22, 1840, SHC.

24. Bartholomew Fuller, "The Dangers of College Life," 1851, Bartholomew Fuller Papers, SHC.

25. Dabney, *Mr. Jefferson's University*, 21.

26. Diary of Basil Manly II (no. 3, 1843–1848), January 29, 1848, Manly Family Papers, UA.

27. L. Ray Drinkwater, "Honor and Student Misconduct in Southern Antebellum Colleges," *Southern Humanities Review* 27 (fall 1993): 330; J. F. Henry to Tadry Henry, November 23, 1856, Gustavus A. Henry Papers, SHC.

28. R. L. Dabney to Elizabeth Dabney, June 14, 1836, Papers of the Dabney Family, UVA-Alderman.

29. R. L. Dabney to Charles W. Dabney, August 1, 1837, ibid.

30. James Gwyn Diary, October 2, 1850, SHC.

31. James I. Robertson Jr., *Stonewall Jackson: The Man, the Soldier, the Legend* (New York: Macmillan, 1997), 124.

32. William Gibson Field Journal [typescript], p. 5, UVA-Wilson.

33. G. K. Miller to Cellie McCann, November 6, 1860, George Knox Miller Papers, SHC.

34. R. L. Dabney to Elizabeth Dabney, June 8, 1836, Papers of the Dabney Family, UVA-Alderman.

35. John D. Wright Jr., *Transylvania: Tutor to the West* (Lexington, Ky.: Univ. Press of Kentucky, 1975), 96; William Sydney Mullins Diary, January 29, 1841, SHC; Ollinger Crenshaw, *General Lee's College: The Rise and Growth of Washington and Lee University* (New York: Random House, 1969), 107.

36. Quoted in James Allen Cabaniss, *The University of Mississippi: Its First Hundred Years,* 2nd ed. (Hattiesburg: Univ. College Press of Mississippi, 1971), 28.

37. A. M. McCollam Jr. to Father, March 6, 1860, Andrew McCollam Papers, SHC.

38. Diary of Basil Manly II (no. 4, 1848–1857), p. 28, Manly Family Papers, UA.

39. R. L. Dabney to Elizabeth Dabney, February 19, 1837, Papers of the Dabney Family, UVA-Alderman.

40. R. L. Dabney to Elizabeth Dabney, June 8, 1836, ibid.

41. R. L. Dabney to Elizabeth Dabney, November 9, 1836, ibid.

42. Quoted in James Edward Scanlon, *Randolph-Macon College: A Southern History, 1825–1967* (Charlottesville: Univ. Press of Virginia, 1983), 80.

43. R. L. Dabney to Charles W. Dabney, August 5, 1836, Papers of the Dabney Family, UVA-Alderman; William Sydney Mullins Diary, January 29, 1841, SHC.

44. Quoted in Scanlon, *Randolph-Macon College,* 73.

45. James Gwyn Diary, September 6, 1850, SHC.

46. Ibid., September 11, 1850.

47. Quoted in Tolbert, ed., *Two Hundred Years,* 31.

48. For a discussion of the role of southern honor and male sexual conquest, see Bertram Wyatt-Brown, *Southern Honor: Ethics and Behavior in the Old South* (New York and Oxford: Oxford Univ. Press, 1982), 292–324.

49. G. F. Dabney to Elizabeth Dabney, February 23, 1840, Papers of the Dabney Family, UVA-Alderman; Diary of Basil Manly II (no. 3, 1843–1848), February 19, 1845, Manly Family Papers, UA.

50. Robert Whitehead to Floyd L. Whitehead, March 18, 1833, Papers of Floyd L. Whitehead, UVA-Alderman.

51. R. L. Dabney to Elizabeth Dabney, September 10, 1834, Papers of the Dabney Family, UVA-Alderman.

52. William Blackledge Whitfield Diary, March 31, 1860, William Blackledge Whitfield Papers, SHC.

53. Dabney, *Mr. Jefferson's University*, 21.

54. Quoted in Cummins, *Austin College*, 47.

55. William H. Burwell to Mother, February 12, 1853, Boyd Family Papers, SHC; Leonidas Siler to Sallie Jarrett, May 25, 1850, Sarah A. Jarrett Papers, SHC.

56. Arthur McKimmon to Sophie Manly, October 28 and November 15 and 20, 1859, Manly Family Papers, SHC.

57. William Sydney Mullins Diary, June 2–3, 1841, SHC.

58. Leonidas Siler to Sallie Jarrett, October 13, 1850, Sarah A. Jarrett Papers, SHC.

59. George Penn to Eliza Penn, January 5, 1842, Elizabeth Seawell Penn Hairston Papers, SHC.

60. Wyatt-Brown, *Southern Honor*, 295.

61. R. L. Dabney to Woodson Payne, March 18, 1840, Dabney Family Papers, SHC.

62. Quoted in Carol Bleser, ed., *Secret and Sacred: The Diaries of James Henry Hammond, a Southern Slaveholder* (New York and Oxford: Oxford Univ. Press, 1988), 5.

63. D. B. DeSaussure to Charles J. Stroman, July 27, 1854, Charles J. Stroman Letters, DU.

64. Ibid.

65. Chas. Minor Blackford to Launcelot M. Blackford, March 4, 1852, Launcelot Minor Blackford Letters, SHC.

66. Leonidas Siler to Sallie Jarrett, April 9, 1850, Sarah A. Jarrett Papers, SHC.

67. Quoted in William Hamilton Nelson, *A Burning Torch and a Flaming Fire: The Story of Centenary College of Louisiana* (Nashville, Tenn.: Methodist Publishing House, 1931), 145.

4. HONOR AND VIOLENCE

1. Maximilian La Borde, *History of the South Carolina College, From Its Incorporation December 19, 1801, to Nov. 25, 1857, Including Sketches of Its Presidents and Professors* (Columbia, S.C.: Peter B. Glass, 1859), 278–9.

2. Herbert Clarence Bradshaw, *History of Hampden-Sydney College: Volume 1, From the Beginnings to the Year 1856* (Durham, N.C.: Seeman Printery, 1976), 127–8.

3. "Rules and Regulations, East Alabama Male College" [typescript], Misc. collection, Series 1, AU.

4. Diary of Basil Manly II (no. 3, 1843–1848), November 11 and 15, 1843, and January 27, 1847, Manly Family Papers, UA. See also pp. 1–2.

5. Ibid., January 31 and February 15, 1844.

6. Abner Stith to Thomas Jones, March 31, 1814, Thomas Williamson Jones Letters, SHC.

7. Bradshaw, *History of Hampden-Sydney College*, 118.

8. Virginius Dabney, *Mr. Jefferson's University: A History* (Charlottesville: Univ. Press of Virginia, 1981), 8–9.

9. La Borde, *History of the South Carolina College,* 276–7.

10. L. Ray Drinkwater, "Honor and Student Misconduct in Southern Antebellum Colleges," *Southern Humanities Review* 27 (fall 1993): 337.

11. A. L. Pickens to Samuel Pickens [typescript], March 9, 1835, Pickens Family Papers, ADAH.

12. *Report of the Committee of Investigation Who Were Instructed to Enquire into the Causes Which Have Produced the Late Disturbances and Decline of the University of Alabama* (Tuskaloosa: M. D. J. Slade, 1837), 6–7.

13. Ibid., 7–9.

14. Lisa Tolbert, ed., *Two Hundred Years of Student Life at Chapel Hill: Selected Letters and Diaries* (Chapel Hill, N.C.: Center for the Study of the American South, IRSS Faculty Working Group in Southern Studies, 1993), 70.

15. William Sydney Mullins Diary, January 19, 1841, SHC.

16. George Penn to Thomas Penn, November 15, 1842, Elizabeth Seawell Penn Hairston Papers, SHC.

17. R. L. Dabney to G. W. Payne, November 15, 1840, and R. L. Dabney to Elizabeth Dabney, December 7, 1840, Papers of the Dabney Family, UVA-Alderman.

18. Diary of Basil Manly II (no. 3, 1843–1848), January 26, 1848; James B. Sellers, *History of the University of Alabama, Vol. I, 1818–1902* (University: Univ. of Alabama Press, 1953), 241–2.

19. Diary of Basil Manly II (No. 3, 1843–1848), January 26, 1848.

20. F. W. Harrison to Thomas Jones, March 3, 1823, Thomas Williamson Jones Letters, SHC.

21. R. L. Dabney to Elizabeth Dabney, March 30, 1837, Papers of the Dabney Family, UVA-Alderman.

22. Tolbert, ed., *Two Hundred Years,* 64.

23. James Allen Cabaniss, *The University of Mississippi: Its First Hundred Years,* 2nd ed. (Hattiesburg: Univ. College Press of Mississippi, 1971), 49–50.

24. Diary of Basil Manly II (no. 3, 1843–1848), October 23, 1846, Manly Family Papers, UA.

25. William Sydney Mullins Diary, October 28, 1840, SHC.

26. Ibid., November 17 and 20, 1840.

5. COLLEGE LIFE AND THE CIVIL WAR

1. Ollinger Crenshaw, *General Lee's College: The Rise and Growth of Washington and Lee University* (New York: Random House, 1969), 119.

2. Ibid., 120–4.

3. Andrew McCollam Jr. to Father, October 10 and November 23, 1860, Andrew McCollam Papers, SHC.

4. Ibid.

5. G. K. Miller to Cellie McCann, November 24, 1860, and December 13, 1860, George Knox Miller Papers, SHC.

6. John Luster Brinkley, *On This Hill: A Narrative History of Hampden-Sydney College, 1774–1994* (Hampden-Sydney, Va.: [Hampden-Sydney College], 1994), 273.

7. Walter C. Preston to John M. Preston Sr., April 29, 1861, Virginiana Collection, UVA-Alderman.

8. Andrew McCollam Jr. to Father, April 18, 1861, Andrew McCollam Papers, SHC.

9. Frank L. Little, "Reminiscences," October 23, 1911, AU.

10. Quoted in William Hamilton Nelson, *A Burning Torch and a Flaming Fire: The Story of Centenary College of Louisiana* (Nashville, Tenn.: Methodist Publishing House, 1931), 172–3.

11. Thomas K. Hearn Jr., *Wake Forest and the Spirit of Opportunity* (New York: Newcomen Society of the United States, 1984), 15.

12. William Edward Eisenberg, *The First Hundred Years, Roanoke College, 1842–1942* (Salem, Va.: Trustees of Roanoke College, 1942), 93.

13. Walter C. Preston to John M. Preston Sr., April 29, 1861, Virginiana Collection, UVA-Alderman.

14. Macon Abernathy to Sister, February 24, 1861, Macon and Miles W. Abernathy Letters, UA.

15. Brinkley, *On This Hill,* 273–6.

16. James B. Sellers, *History of the University of Alabama, Vol. I, 1818–1902* (University: Univ. of Alabama Press, 1953), 258–65.

17. Andrew McCollam to Mother, January 20, 1861, Andrew McCollam Papers, SHC.

18. James Allen Cabaniss, *The University of Mississippi: Its First Hundred Years,* 2nd ed. (Hattiesburg: Univ. College Press of Mississippi, 1971), 50–2.

19. Brinkley, *On This Hill,* 276–88.

20. Report of Lt. Col. Scott Shipp, "Battle of New Market, Virginia, and Aftermath," July 4, 1864, VMI; Gen. Francis H. Smith, "Report on the Battle of New Market, Virginia, and Aftermath," *VMI Annual Report* (July 1864), 21–3, VMI.

21. Eisenberg, *First Hundred Years,* 97–8.

22. Gratz Cohen to Papa, June 10, 1862, and Gratz Cohen to Parents, May 11, 1862, Miriam Gratz Moses Cohen Papers, SHC.

23. Gratz Cohen to Papa, May 7, 1863, Miriam Gratz Moses Cohen Papers, SHC.

24. L. M. Blackford to Mrs. Wm. M. Blackford, July 21, 1861, Launcelot Minor Blackford Letters, UVA-Alderman.

25. Cornelius Dabney Diary, December 13, 1863, SHC.

26. Gratz Cohen to Papa, October 22, 1862; Gratz Cohen to Papa, October 19, 1862; and Gratz Cohen to Papa and Mama, June 22, 1862, Miriam Gratz Moses Cohen Papers, SHC.

27. Reuben W. Boling to Mary A. Boling, November 8, 1864, James M. Boling Papers, UA.

28. Cornelius Dabney Diary, November 9 and October 12, 1863, SHC.

29. Quoted in Brinkley, *On This Hill,* 290.

30. Quoted ibid., 289.

31. Eisenberg, *First Hundred Years,* 95–106.

32. Sellers, *History of the University of Alabama,* 264–7.

33. Francis Smith, "The Burning of the Virginia Military Institute," *VMI Annual Report* (July 1864), VMI.

34. Sellers, *History of the University of Alabama,* 279–86.

35. Peter W. Bardaglio, *Reconstructing the Household: Families, Sex, and the Law in the Nineteenth-Century South,* Studies in Legal History, edited by Thomas A. Green and Hendrik Hartog (Chapel Hill: Univ. of North Carolina Press, 1995), 5.

36. Bertram Wyatt-Brown, *Southern Honor: Ethics and Behavior in the Old South* (New York and Oxford: Oxford Univ. Press, 1982), xii, xv.

37. Kenneth S. Greenberg, *Honor and Slavery: Lies, Duels, Noses, Masks, Dressing as a Woman, Gifts, Strangers, Humanitarianism, Death, Slave Rebellions, the Proslavery Argument, Baseball, Hunting, and Gambling in the Old South* (Princeton, N.J.: Princeton Univ. Press, 1996), 62.

Bibliography

UNPUBLISHED PRIMARY SOURCES

Alabama Department of Archives and History, Montgomery, Alabama.
   Sarah Lowe Diaries.
   James Osgood Andrew Story Diary.
   Pickens Family Papers (Andrew L. Pickens Papers).
   Tait Family Papers (Dr. Charles W. Tait Papers).
   Henry Watson Diary.
   Webb Family Papers.

Special Collections, Auburn University Library, Auburn, Alabama.
   Fred Allison Papers.
   William Leroy Broun Papers.
   B. C. Lee Letter [typescript].
   Frank L. Little, "Reminiscences."

Special Collections Library, Duke University, Durham, North Carolina.
   Major Bell Letters.
   John Marshall Clement Papers.
   Davis Family Correspondence.
   Enoch Faw Diary.
   Thomas Wingfield Grimes Papers.
   William Haynie Hatchett Letters.
   William A. Hightower Letters.
   Philip H. Howerton Papers.
   Charles H. Hunton Papers.
   Laura C. Kemp Papers.

W. Robert Leckie Papers.

Ranson Lee Papers.

John Bowie Magruder Papers.

Melchizedek Spragins Correspondence.

Charles J. Stroman Letters.

Cabell Tavender Papers.

Thomas White Papers.

Georgia Historical Society, Savannah, Georgia.

Wayne-Stites-Anderson Papers.

Southern Historical Collection, University of North Carolina at Chapel Hill.

D. Wyatt Aiken Autobiography [typescript].

Belle Atkinson Papers.

Blackford Family Manuscripts.

B. Lewis Blackford Letters.

Launcelot Minor Blackford Letters.

Boyd Family Papers.

Mary Biddle Norcott Bryan Scrapbook.

Miriam Gratz Moses Cohen Papers.

Edmund Strudwick Burwell Papers.

John Caldwell Papers.

Rufus Lawrence Coffin Album.

Cornelius Dabney Diary [typescript].

William Porcher Dubose Reminiscences.

Bartholomew Fuller Papers.

Haywood W. Guion Papers.

James Gwyn Diary.

William H. Haigh Papers.

Elizabeth Seawell Penn Hairston Papers.

Gustavus A. Henry Papers.

Robert Philip Howell Memoirs [typescript].

Sally Long Jarman Papers.

Sarah A. Jarrett Papers.

Thomas Williamson Jones Letters.

Manly Family Papers.

John S. Martin Papers.

David McMichen Lees Papers.

McBee Family Papers.

Andrew McCollam Papers.

Anna R. McIver Papers.

Hector James McNeill Letters.

George Knox Miller Papers.

Miriam Gratz Moses Papers.

William Sydney Mullins Diary.

Neal Family Papers.

Satterfield and Merritt Family Papers.

Skinner Family Papers.

John Dudley Tatum Letters.

Nathan Wilson Walker Papers.

Harvey Walter Washington Papers.

Henry Young Webb Diary and Letter.

William Blackledge Whitfield Papers.

James Gwyn Papers.

Isaac Barton Ulmer Papers.

Hoole Library Special Collections, University of Alabama, Tuscaloosa, Alabama.

Macon and Miles W. Abernathy Letters.

James M. Boling Papers.

John Little Letters.

Manly Family Papers.

Marr-Carson-McCormick Papers.

W. C. L. Richardson Letters.

Ross-Searcy-Snow Papers.

John Gill Shorter Papers.

Walker-Reese Papers.

Alderman Library Special Collections, University of Virginia, Charlottesville, Virginia.

Aylett Family Papers.

Papers of the Barbour and Related Fields Families.

John Bell Papers (microfilm).

Blackford Family Manuscripts.

Launcelot Minor Blackford Letters.

Papers of the Dabney Family.

Papers of the Hunter-Garnett Families.

Joel Leftwich Papers.

Papers of the McCue Family.

Virginiana Collection.

Papers of Floyd L. Whitehead.

Wilson Library, University of Virginia, Charlottesville, Virginia.

William Gibson Field Journal [typescript].

Virginia Military Institute Archives, Virginia Military Institute, Lexington, Virginia.

Report of Lt. Col. Scott Shipp, "Battle of New Market, Virginia, and Aftermath."

VMI Annual Report, 1863 and 1864.

PUBLISHED PRIMARY SOURCES

Alabama Legislature, Committee on the State University. *Report.* Montgomery, Ala.: McCormick and Walshe, 1848.

Bleser, Carol, ed. *Secret and Sacred: The Diaries of James Henry Hammond, a Southern Slaveholder.* New York and Oxford: Oxford Univ. Press, 1988.

Bondurant, Emily. *Reminiscences.* N.p., privately printed, 1962.

Chamberlain, Hope Summerell, ed. *Old Days in Chapel Hill: Being the Life and Letters of Cornelia Phillips Spencer.* Chapel Hill: Univ. of North Carolina Press, 1926.

Collier, H. W. *To the Citizens of Alabama.* Tuscaloosa, Ala.: n.p., 1850.

Connor, R. D. W., ed. *A Documentary History of the University of North Carolina, 1776–1799.* Chapel Hill: Univ. of North Carolina Press, 1953.

Deems, Charles Force. *Autobiography.* New York: Fleming H. Revell, 1897.

Griffith, Lucille Blanche. *History of Alabama, 1540–1900; As Recorded in the Diaries, Letters, and Papers of the Time.* Northport, Ala.: Colonial Press, 1962.

Report of the Committee of Investigation Who Were Instructed to Enquire into the Causes Which Have Produced the Late Disturbances and Decline of the University of Alabama. Tuskaloosa: M. D. J. Slade, 1837.

"Rules and Regulations, East Alabama Male College" [typescript]. Misc. collection, Series 1, AU.

Schmandt, Raymond H., and Josephine H. Schulte, eds. *A Civil War Diary: The Diary of Spring Hill College between the Years, 1861–1865.* Mobile, Ala.: Spring Hill College Press, 1982.

Sullins, David. *Recollections of an Old Man: Seventy Years in Dixie, 1827–1897.* Bristol, Tenn.: King Printing Co., 1910.

Taylor, Joe. *A Plea for the University of Alabama: An Address Delivered before the Erosophic and Philomathic Societies of the University of Alabama on Their Anniversary Occasion, August 9, 1847.* Tuscaloosa: M. D. J. Slade, 1847.

Tolbert, Lisa, ed. *Two Hundred Years of Student Life at Chapel Hill: Selected Letters and Diaries.* Chapel Hill, N.C.: Center for the Study of the American South, IRSS Faculty Working Group in Southern Studies, 1993.

Tomes, Robert. *My College Days.* New York: Harper, 1880.

University of South Carolina. *War Records.* Columbia: n.p., 1907–08.

Woods, Alva. *Valedictory Address, Delivered December 6, 1837: At the Close of the Seventh Collegiate Year of the University of the State of Alabama.* Tuscaloosa: Marmaduke J. Slade, 1837.

SECONDARY SOURCES

Akers, Samuel Luttrell. *The First Hundred Years of Wesleyan College, 1836–1936.* Savannah: Beehive Press, 1976.

Alley, Reuben E. *History of the University of Richmond, 1830–1871.* Charlottesville: Univ. Press of Virginia, 1983.

Allmendinger, David F. *Paupers and Scholars: The Transformation of Student Life in Nineteenth-Century New England.* New York: St. Martin's Press, 1975.

Bardaglio, Peter W. *Reconstructing the Household: Families, Sex, and the Law in the Nineteenth-Century South.* Studies in Legal History. Edited by Thomas A. Green and Hendrik Hartog. Chapel Hill: Univ. of North Carolina Press, 1995.

Battle, Kemp P. *History of the University of North Carolina.* Raleigh, N.C.: Edwards and Broughton Printing, 1907–1912.

Bell, Sadie. *The Church, the State, and Education in Virginia.* 1930. Reprint, New York: Arno Press, 1969.

Blair, Carolyn L., and Arda S. Walker. *By Faith Endowed: The Story of Maryville College, 1819–1994.* Maryville, Tenn.: Maryville College Press, 1994.

Blandin, I. M. E. *History of Higher Education of Women in the South Prior to*

1860. New York and Washington, D.C.: Neale, 1909. Reprint, Washington, D.C.: Zenger, 1975.

Bond, Oliver James. *The Story of the Citadel*. Richmond, Va.: Garrett and Massie, 1936. Reprint, Greenville, S.C.: Southern Historical Press, 1982.

Bone, Winstead Paine. *A History of Cumberland University, 1842–1935*. Lebanon, Tenn.: The Author, 1935.

Boyle, Charles J. *Twice Remembered: Moments in the History of Spring Hill College*. Mobile, Ala.: Friends of the Spring Hill College Library, 1993.

Bradshaw, Herbert Clarence. *History of Hampden-Sydney College: Vol. 1, From the Beginnings to the Year 1856*. Durham, N.C.: Seeman Printery, 1976.

Brinkley, John Luster. *On This Hill: A Narrative History of Hampden-Sydney College, 1774–1994*. Hampden-Sydney, Va.: [Hampden-Sydney College], 1994.

Bruce, Philip Alexander. *History of the University of Virginia, 1819–1919: The Lengthened Shadow of One Man*. 5 vols. New York: Macmillan, 1920–1922.

Bullock, Henry Morton. *A History of Emory University*. Atlanta: Cherokee, 1972.

Button, H. Warren, and Eugene F. Provenzo Jr. *History of Education and Culture in America*. Englewood Cliffs, N.J.: Prentice-Hall, 1983.

Cabaniss, James Allen. *A History of the University of Mississippi*. University: University of Mississippi, 1949.

———. *The University of Mississippi: Its First Hundred Years*, 2nd ed. Hattiesburg: Univ. College Press of Mississippi, 1971.

Chaffin, Nora Campbell. *Trinity College, 1839–1932: The Beginnings of Duke University*. Durham: Duke Univ. Press, 1950.

Chitty, Arthur Ben. *Reconstruction at Sewanee: The Founding of the University of the South and Its First Administration, 1857–1872*. Sewanee, Tenn.: Univ. Press, 1954.

Clinton, Catherine. *The Plantation Mistress: Woman's World in the Old South*. New York: Pantheon, 1982.

Cohen, Dov, Joseph Vandello, and Adrian K. Rantilla. "The Sacred and the Social: Honor and Violence in Cultural Context." In *Shame: Interpersonal Behavior, Psychopathology, and Culture*, edited by Paul Gilbert and Bernice Andrews. Series in Affective Science. Cambridge: Oxford Univ. Press, 1998.

Cook, Harvey Toliver. *Education in South Carolina under Baptist Control*. Greenville, S.C.: n.p., 1912.

Corley, Robert G., and Samuel N. Stayer. *View from the Hilltop: The First 125*

Years of Birmingham-Southern College. Birmingham, Ala.: Birmingham-Southern College, 1981.

Coulter, E. Merton. *College Life in the Old South: As Seen at the University of Georgia.* New York: Macmillan, 1928. Reprint, Athens: Univ. of Georgia Press, 1983.

Crenshaw, Ollinger. *General Lee's College: The Rise and Growth of Washington and Lee University.* New York: Random House, 1969.

Cummings, A. W. *The Early Schools of Methodism.* New York: Phillips and Hunt, Cincinnati: Cranston and Stowe, 1886.

Cummins, Light Townsend. *Austin College: A Sesquicentennial History, 1849–1999.* Austin: Eakin Press, 1999.

———, ed. *Sociable Scholars: Informal Essays on the History of Student Life at Austin College.* Sherman: Austin College Press, 1990.

Dabney, Virginius. *America's Bicentennial '76 College: The Story of Hampden-Sydney College in Virginia.* New York: Newcomen Society in North America, 1973.

———. *Mr. Jefferson's University: A History.* Charlottesville: Univ. Press of Virginia, 1981.

———. *Virginia Commonwealth University: A Sesquicentennial History.* Charlottesville: Univ. Press of Virginia, 1987.

Daniel, Robert Norman. *Furman University, A History.* Greenville, S.C.: Furman University, 1951.

Daniel, W. Harrison. "Old Lynchburg College, 1855–1869." *Virginia Magazine of History and Biography* 88, no. 4 (October 1980): 446–77.

Davis, Thomas W., ed. *A Crowd of Honorable Youths: Historical Essays on the First 150 Years of the Virginia Military Institute.* Lexington: VMI Alumni Association, 1988.

Dedmond, Francis B. *Catawba: The Story of a College.* Boone, N.C.: Arromondt House, 1989.

Dew, Lee A., and Richard Weiss. *In Pursuit of a Dream: A History of Kentucky Wesleyan College.* Owensboro: Kentucky Wesleyan College Press, 1992.

Dowell, Spright. *A History of Mercer University, 1833–1953.* Macon: Mercer University, 1958.

Drake, William Earle. *Higher Education in NC before 1860.* New York: G. W. Carleton, 1964.

Drinkwater, L. Ray. "Honor and Student Misconduct in Southern Antebellum Colleges." *Southern Humanities Review* 27 (fall 1993): 323–44.

Durrill, Wayne K. "The Power of Ancient Words: Classical Teaching and Social Change at South Carolina College, 1804–1860." *Journal of Southern History* 65, no. 3 (August 1999): 469–98.

Duvall, Sylvanus Milne. *The Methodist Episcopal Church and Education up to 1869.* New York: Bureau of Publications, Teacher College, Columbia University, 1928.

Dyer, John P. *Tulane: The Biography of a University, 1834–1965.* New York: Harper and Row, 1966.

Dyer, Thomas G. *The University of Georgia: A Bicentennial History, 1785–1985.* Athens: Univ. of Georgia Press, 1985.

Eisenberg, William Edward. *The First Hundred Years, Roanoke College, 1842–1942.* Salem, Va.: Trustees of Roanoke College, 1942.

Ellison, Rhonda Coleman. *History of Huntingdon College, 1854–1954.* University: Univ. of Alabama Press, 1954.

Faragher, John Mack, and Florence Howe, eds. *Women and Higher Education in American History: Essays from the Mount Holyoke College Sesquicentennial Symposia.* New York and London: W. W. Norton, 1988.

Farnham, Christie Anne. *The Education of the Southern Belle: Higher Education and Student Socialization in the Antebellum South.* New York and London: New York Univ. Press, 1994.

Faust, Drew Gilpin. *James Henry Hammond and the Old South: A Design for Mastery.* Baton Rouge and London: Louisiana State Univ. Press, 1982.

Fay, Edwin Whitfield. *The History of Education in Louisiana.* Washington, D.C.: Government Printing Office, 1898.

Folmsbee, Stanley John. *East Tennessee University, 1840–1879: Predecessor of the University of Tennessee.* Knoxville: Univ. of Tennessee Press, 1959.

Fox-Genovese, Elizabeth. *Within the Plantation Household: Black and White Women in the Old South.* Chapel Hill: Univ. of North Carolina Press, 1988.

Fries, Adelaide F. *Historical Sketch of Salem Female Academy.* Salem, N.C.: Crist and Keehn, Printers, 1902.

Gallalee, John M. *The University of Alabama: A Short History.* New York: Newcomen Society in North America, 1953.

Godbold, Albea. *The Church College of the Old South.* Durham, N.C.: Duke Univ. Press, 1944.

Goode, James M. "A Rowdy Beginning, an Unusual History: The Jefferson Society from 1825 to 1865." *University of Virginia Magazine* 125 (December 1965), 7–10.

Graves, Thomas Ashley. *The College of William and Mary in Virginia.* New York: Newcomen Society in America, 1976.

Green, Edwin L. *A History of the University of South Carolina.* Columbia: The State, 1916.

Greenberg, Kenneth S. *Honor and Slavery: Lies, Duels, Noses, Masks, Dressing as a Woman, Gifts, Strangers, Humanitarianism, Death, Slave Rebellions, the Proslavery Argument, Baseball, Hunting, and Gambling in the Old South.* Princeton, N.J.: Princeton Univ. Press, 1996.

Griffin, Anne Frierson. *Columbia College Centennial: An Historical Pageant.* Columbia, S.C.: Farrell Press, 1956.

Guilford College, History Committee. *The Story of Guilford College, Told by the History Committee.* Guilford, N.C.: Guilford College, 1934.

Hamilton, Frances Dew, and Elizabeth Crabtree Wells. *Daughters of the Dream: Judson College, 1838–1988.* Marion, Ala.: Judson College, 1989.

Handlin, Oscar, and Mary F. Handlin. *The American College and American Culture.* New York: McGraw-Hill, 1970.

Hanft, Sheldon. "Mordecai's Female Academy." *American Jewish History* 79 (autumn 1989): 72–93.

Harding, Thomas S. *College Literary Societies: Their Contributions to Higher Education in the United States.* New York: Pageant Press International, 1971.

Hearn, Thomas K., Jr. *Wake Forest and the Spirit of Opportunity.* New York: Newcomen Society of the United States, 1984.

Heatwole, Cornelius. *A History of Education in Virginia.* New York: Macmillan, 1916.

Heilman, E. Bruce. *The Story of the University of Richmond: A Sesquicentennial Address.* New York: Newcomen Society in North America, 1979.

The History of Transylvania University, 1780–1909. Louisville: Rafinesque Press, 1969.

Hollis, Daniel Walker. *University of South Carolina.* 2 vols. Columbia: Univ. of South Carolina Press, 1951–1956.

Horowitz, Helen Lefkowitz. *Campus Life: Undergraduate Cultures from the End of the Eighteenth Century to the Present.* Chapel Hill: Univ. of North Carolina Press, 1995.

Huddle, Orlando Earhardt. *A History of Georgetown College.* Master's thesis, University of Kentucky, 1930.

Jennings, Walter Wilson. *Transylvania: Pioneer University of the West.* New York: Pageant Press, 1955.

Jones, Ralph Wood. *Southwestern University, 1840–1961.* Austin: Jenkins, 1973.

Jordan, Ervin L. *Charlottesville and the University of Virginia in the Civil War.* Lynchburg, Va.: H. E. Howard, 1988.

Kenny, Michael. *Catholic Culture in Alabama: Centenary Story of Spring Hill College, 1830–1930.* New York: America Press, 1931.

Kett, Joseph F. *Rites of Passage: Adolescence in America, 1790 to the Present.* New York: Basic Books, 1977.

La Borde, Maximilian. *History of the South Carolina College, From Its Incorporation December 19, 1801, to Nov. 25, 1857, Including Sketches of Its Presidents and Professors.* Columbia, S.C.: Peter B. Glass, 1859.

Landolt, George L. *Search for the Summit: Austin College through XII Decades, 1849–1970.* Sherman: Austin College Alumni Association, 1970.

Leland, Jack. *200 Years of Academic Excellence: College of Charleston, 1785–1985.* Charleston, S.C.: College of Charleston, 1985.

Leonard, Jacob Calvin. *History of Catawba College.* Lexington, N.C.: n.p., 1927.

Limestone College. *The Centennial of Limestone College, Nov. 6, 1845 to Nov. 5, 1945.* Gaffney, S.C., 1945.

Lipset, Seymour Martin, and Philip G. Altbach, eds. *Students in Revolt.* Boston: Houghton Mifflin, 1969.

Lloyd, Ralph Waldo. *Maryville College: A History of 150 Years, 1819–1869.* Maryville: Maryville College Press, 1969.

Longenecker, Herbert Eugene. *Great Vision, Amply Justified: The Story of Tulane University.* New York: Newcomen Society in North America, 1968.

Lyon, E. Wilson. "The University in the South." *Virginia Quarterly Review* 44 (summer 1968): 458–69.

Lyon, Ralph M. *A History of Livingston University, 1835–1963.* Livingston, Ala.: [Lyon], 1976.

Manly, Louise. *History of Judson College.* Atlanta: Foote and Davies, [1913?].

Matthews, Jack. "Good Old Ways in the Good Old Days." *Southern Review* 30 (winter 1994): 126–35.

McEwen, Mildred Morse. *Queens College Yesterday and Today.* Charlotte: Queens College Alumnae Association, 1980.

McKnight, Edgar V., and Oscar Creech. *A History of Chowan College*. Murfreesboro: Chowan College, 1964.

McLachlan, James. "The American College in the Nineteenth Century: Toward a Reappraisal." *Teachers' College Record* 80, no. 2 (December 1978): 287–306.

McLeod, John Angus. *From These Stones: Mars Hill College, 1856–1968*. Mars Hill: Mars Hill College, 1968.

McLin, Elva Bell. *Athens State College: A Definitive History, 1821–1991*. Athens, Ala.: Athens State College Foundation, 1991.

McWhiney, Grady. *Cracker Culture: Celtic Ways in the Old South*. Tuscaloosa: Univ. of Alabama Press, 1988.

Menk, Patricia H. *To Live in Time: The Sesquicentennial History of Mary Baldwin College, 1842–1992*. Verona, Va.: Mid Valley Press, 1992.

Meyer, Leland Winfield. *Georgetown College: Its Background and a Chapter in Its Early History*. Louisville: Western Recorder, 1929.

Miller, Howard. *The Revolutionary College: American Presbyterian Higher Education*. New York: New York Univ. Press, 1976.

Miller, Mark F. *"Dear Old Roanoke": A Sesquicentennial Portrait, 1842–1992*. Macon, Ga.: Mercer Univ. Press, 1992.

Montgomery, James Riley, Stanley J. Folmsbee, and Lee Seifert Greene. *To Foster Knowledge: A History of the University of Tennessee, 1794–1970*. Knoxville: Univ. of Tennessee Press, 1984.

Morison, Samuel Eliot. *Three Centuries of Harvard, 1636–1836*. Cambridge, Mass.: Harvard Univ. Press, 1936.

Murphy, Walter Young. *LaGrange College: Georgia's Oldest Independent School*. New York: Newcomen Society of the United States, 1985.

Nelson, William Hamilton. *A Burning Torch and a Flaming Fire: The Story of Centenary College of Louisiana*. Nashville, Tenn.: Methodist Publishing House, 1931.

Nobles, Lewis. *A College for Mississippians: The Story of Mississippi College*. New York: Newcomen Society in North America, 1976.

Novak, Steven J. *The Rights of Youth: American College and Student Revolt, 1798–1815*. Cambridge, Mass., and London: Harvard Univ. Press, 1977.

Pace, Robert F., and Christopher J. Bjornsen. "Adolescent Honor and College Student Behavior in the Old South," *Southern Cultures* 6 (fall 2000), 9–28.

Parks, Joseph Howard, and Oliver C. Weaver Jr. *Birmingham-Southern College, 1856–1956*. Nashville, Tenn.: Parthenon Press, 1957.

Paschal, George Washington. *History of Wake Forest College.* 3 vols. Wake Forest, N.C.: Wake Forest College, 1935–1943.

Peck, Elisabeth Sinclair. *Berea's First Century, 1855–1955.* Lexington: Univ. of Kentucky Press, 1955.

———. *Berea's First 125 Years, 1855–1980.* Lexington: Univ. Press of Kentucky, 1982.

Ragan, Allan Edgar. *A History of Tusculum College, 1794–1944.* Greenville, Tenn.: Tusculum Sesquicentennial Committee, 1945.

Robertson, James I., Jr., *Stonewall Jackson: The Man, the Soldier, the Legend.* New York : Macmillan, 1997.

Rudolph, Frederick. *The American College and University: A History.* New York: Vintage Books, 1962.

———. *Curriculum: A History of the American Undergraduate Course of Study since 1636.* San Francisco: Jossey-Bass, 1977.

Russell, Phillips. *The Woman Who Rang the Bell: The Story of Cornelia Phillips Spencer.* Chapel Hill: Univ. of North Carolina Press, 1949.

Scanlon, James Edward. *Randolph-Macon College: A Southern History, 1825–1967.* Charlottesville: Univ. Press of Virginia, 1983.

Scott, Anne Firor. "The Ever Widening Circle: The Diffusion of Feminist Values at the Troy Female Seminary, 1822–1872." *History of Education Quarterly* 19, no. 1 (spring 1979): 3–25.

Sellers, James B. *History of the University of Alabama, Vol. I, 1818–1902.* University: Univ. of Alabama Press, 1953.

Sheldon, Henry D. *Student Life and Customs.* 1901. Reprint, New York: Arno Press, 1969.

Smith, Andrew C. *The Phoenix and the Turtle: Some Highlights on the History of Spring Hill College.* Mobile, Ala.: Spring Hill College Press, 1957.

Snider, William D. *Light on the Hill: A History of the University of North Carolina at Chapel Hill.* Chapel Hill: Univ. of North Carolina Press, 1992.

Solomon, Barbara Miller. *In the Company of Educated Women: A History of Women and Higher Education in America.* New Haven and London: Yale Univ. Press, 1985.

Sprague, Rosemary. *Longwood College: A History.* Richmond: William Byrd Press, 1989.

Stevenson, George J. *Increase in Excellence: A History of Emory and Henry College.* New York: Appleton-Century-Crofts, 1963.

Stone, Lawrence, ed. *The University in Society.* 2 vols. Princeton, N.J.: Princeton Univ. Press, 1974.

Sulzby, James Frederick. *Toward a History of Samford University.* Birmingham: Samford Univ. Press, 1986.

Sweet, Leonard I. "The Female Seminary Movement and Woman's Mission in Antebellum America." *Church History* 54 (March 1985): 41–55.

Tankersley, Allen P. *College Life at Old Oglethorpe.* Athens: Univ. of Georgia Press, 1951.

Vickery, Dorothy Scovil. *Hollins College, 1842–1942: An Historical Sketch.* Hollins College, Va.: Hollins College, 1942.

Wallace, David Duncan. *History of Wofford College, 1854–1949.* Nashville, Tenn.: Vanderbilt Univ. Press, 1951.

Watters, Mary. *The History of Mary Baldwin College, 1842–1942: Augusta Female Seminary, Mary Baldwin Seminary, Mary Baldwin College.* Staunton, Va.: Mary Baldwin College, 1942.

White, Michael A. *History of Baylor University, 1845–1861.* Waco: Texian Press, 1968.

Whitescarver, Keith. "Creating Citizens for the Republic: Education in Georgia, 1776–1810." *Journal of the Early Republic* 13 (winter 1993): 455–79.

Wise, Henry A. *Drawing Out the Man: The VMI Story.* Charlottesville: Univ. Press of Virginia, 1978.

Woody, Thomas. *A History of Women's Education in the United States.* 2 vols. New York and Lancaster, Pa.: Science Press, 1929.

Wright, John D., Jr. *Transylvania: Tutor to the West.* Lexington: Univ. Press of Kentucky, 1975.

Wyatt-Brown, Bertram. *Southern Honor: Ethics and Behavior in the Old South.* New York and Oxford: Oxford Univ. Press, 1982.

Index

Fourth of July, 58
France, 102
Fredericksburg, Va., 54
Fuller, Bartholomew, 64

Gambling, 63–64, 87
Garland, Landon C., 105, 114, 115
Garnett, James Mercer, Jr., 17, 26, 27, 38
Garrett, Thomas Miles, 27, 40–41
Georgia, 18, 38, 54, 67, 75, 114
Georgia, University of. *See* University of Georgia
Germany, 102
Gordonsville, Va., 67
Green, Thomas B., 50
Greenberg, Kenneth, 8
Gwyn, James, 24, 49–50, 66, 72–73

Hampden-Sidney College (Virginia), 16, 19, 22, 23, 24, 25, 37–38, 40, 41, 45–46, 48, 52–53, 58, 59–60, 61, 65–66, 67, 69–70, 71, 74, 82–84, 86–87, 90, 93–94, 102, 104–105, 106–107, 110, 112–13, 121n11
Harrison, William Henry, 63–64
Harvard University, 7
Henry, John F., 26, 37, 48, 60, 65
Hill, Champ, 60
Hill, William, 60
Hillsboro, N.C., 61, 76, 90
Hines, Calvin, 30–31
Honor, code of: and cheating, 27–28; and the Civil War, 116–17; and class, 17; and commencement, 32; and literary debating societies, 71–72; defined, 4–9; and use of disguises, 65, 85, 91; peer-designed nature of, 67, 92; and public speaking, 31; and quality of education, 15–16; and sexual conquest, 73, 78; and slavery, 50–51; and student rebelliousness, 6–7, 82–84, 87–89; used in discipline of students, 17, 85–87, 92; and campus violence, 91–97
Horace, 20

Horowitz, Helen Lefkowitz, 2–4
Housing, student, 37–41
Howell, Robert Philip, 15
Hunter, Maj. Gen. David, 114–15
Hunting, 59–60, 61
Huntsville, Tex., 60, 75

Illness, 23–24, 42–45, 54
Independence Day celebrations, 58
Ireland, 102

Jackson, La., 42, 45
Jackson, Thomas J., 18–19, 66–67, 115
Jarrett, Sallie, 75–76
Jefferson, Thomas, 87
Johnson, F. M., 36
Johnston, Gen. Joseph E., 116
Jones, John, 54, 86
Jones, Phil, 67
Jones, Thomas, 86
Junkin, George, 98–100

Kentucky, 36, 43, 45, 53, 59
Killough, James T., 92–93
Kingville, Va., 83

Lander, Samuel, Jr., 32–33
Lane, Joseph, 100
Lee, B. C., 12
Lee, Gen. Robert E., 109, 112, 116
Lee, James, Jr., 14
Lees, David, 57
Lees, Hugh, 57
Lexington, Ky., 36
Lexington, Va., 35, 42, 98, 115
Libraries, 69–70
Lincoln, Abraham, 98–101, 102, 116
Literary societies, 29, 67–72, 94, 117
Little, Frank, 103
Little, George, 12–13
Little, John, 12–13
London Metropolitan, 27

South Carolina, University of. *See* South Carolina College

South Carolina College, 20–21, 65, 78–79, 82–84, 87

Spain, 102

Spencer, P. P., 96

Stanford, Ky., 36

Stith, Abner, 86

Student organizations: fraternities, 4, 107, 117; Prussian *Burschenshaft*, 8; Sons of Temperance, 62, 77. *See also* Literary societies

Students: alcohol use by, 25, 49, 61–62, 87, 90, 111; attitudes about secession, 98–103; attitudes about education, 12–15; as cadets during Civil War, 103–108, 114–16; and cheating, 22, 27–28; and commencement exercises, 28–33, 69, 77; correspondence with, 56–58; courtship and sexuality of, 31, 73–81, 94, 111–12; and dancing, 29, 60, 111; depression among, 44; and dining, 45–47, 110–11, 112, 113; European, 8–9; female, 9–10, 113–14, 117; fishing and hunting by, 59–60, 91; frivolity and frolics among, 58–60, 64–65; gambling by, 63–64, 87; homesickness of, 34, 36–37; illness among, 23–24, 42–45, 54; importance of clothing to, 51–52, 111; and literary societies, 67–72, 94; and living accommodations, 37–41; and military service, 106–108; and money, 29–30, 51–54; northern, 7; pranks by, 6, 18, 58, 65–67, 82–83; and college or university pride, 13–16; relationship to faculty, 6, 16–19, 26; rebelliousness of, 3, 7–8, 26, 74, 86–90, 98–100; and roommates, 24–25, 40, 45, 67; and slavery, 47–51, 54; social classes among, 4, 7, 16–17, 52–53; speeches given by, 24, 29–32, 69–70, 80–81; and studying, 22–25; theatrical exhibitions of, 113–14; tobacco use by, 62–63, 87; travel difficulties of, 34–35;

violence among, 91–96; and weapons, 90–92, 94

Tatum, J. D., 17–18

Taylor, Gen. Richard, 116

Teaching methods: examinations, 20–21; field trips, 23; oration, 21; recitation, 21, 28. *See also* Curriculum

Tennessee, 24, 37

Tobacco, 62–63, 87

Transylvania University (Kentucky), 45, 48, 51–52, 68

Trinity College (North Carolina), 15

Tuscaloosa, Ala., 88–89, 115

Uncle Remus, 112

University of Alabama, 12, 28, 50–51, 58, 65, 69, 73–74, 85–86, 88–90, 92–93, 95, 104, 105–106, 111, 114

University of Georgia, 2

University of Mississippi, 69, 94, 106

University of North Carolina, 1, 14–15, 17, 22–23, 25, 26, 27, 28–29, 31, 34–35, 36–37, 38–39, 40–41, 46, 54, 55, 57, 59, 63, 64, 68–69, 71, 73, 74–77, 80, 86, 90, 91, 93, 94, 95–96

University of South Carolina. *See* South Carolina College

University of Virginia, 14, 16, 18, 26, 37, 39, 42, 43, 44, 45, 47, 48, 52–54, 62, 63, 64–65, 67, 73, 75, 78, 79–80, 87, 88, 91–92, 101–102, 104, 108–11

Virginia, 16, 24, 35, 36, 45, 67, 82, 99–100, 101, 102, 103–104, 107

Virginia, University of. *See* University of Virginia

Virginia Collegiate Institute (later Roanoke College), 14, 34. *See also* Roanoke College (Virginia)

Virginia Military Institute, 18–19, 66–67, 105, 107, 108, 114–15; Corps of Cadets, 107